# TEACH YOURSELF BOOKS

# WRITING
# A ROMANTIC
# NOVEL
*and getting published*

# WRITING A ROMANTIC NOVEL

*and getting published*

**Donna Baker**

TEACH YOURSELF BOOKS

Long renowned as the authoritative source for self-guided learning – with more than 30 million copies sold worldwide – the *Teach Yourself* series includes over 200 titles in the fields of languages, crafts, hobbies, sports, and other leisure activities.

A catalogue record for this title is available from The British Library

*Library of Congress Catalog Card Number on file.*

First published in UK 1997 by Hodder Headline Plc, 338 Euston Road, London NW1 3BH

First published in US 1998 by NTC Publishing Group
An imprint of NTC/Contemporary Publishing Company
4255 West Touhy Avenue, Lincolnwood (Chicago), Illinois 60646·1975 U.S.A.

The 'Teach Yourself' name and logo are registered trade marks of Hodder & Stoughton Ltd in the UK.

Typeset by Hart McLeod, Cambridge.
Printed in England by Cox & Wyman Limited, Reading, Berkshire.

| Impression number | 10 9 8 7 6 5 4 3 2 1 |
|---|---|
| Year | 2000 1999 1998 1997 |

# CONTENTS

# By the same author

# ACKNOWLEDGEMENTS

On behalf of all who read this book, I gratefully thank those listed below, who so generously gave me their own 'tips' to pass on:

Margaret Graham

Marcia Willett

Margaret Thomson Davis

Katie Flynn

Patricia Burns

Jessica Stirling

Sheila Walsh

Dee Williams

Pamela Oldfield

Charlotte Lamb

Jean Saunders
(aka Rowena Summers, Sally Blake)'

Iris Gower

Judy Saxton

Joanna Trollope

Caroline Sheldon

The remains of the original manuscript for this book are now donated to my two ginger kittens, Mustard and Pepper, so that they may perfect the talent for shredding that has become so apparent...

And the book itself is dedicated to all new writers.

May your talents increase.

# INTRODUCTION

> 'I'd like to write a book if only I had the time.'
>
> 'Have you ever thought of writing *real* books?'
>
> 'Romantic novels? I'm afraid I don't read them myself.'
>
> 'Does anyone actually *read* that stuff?'

If you're already a writer, you'll probably have heard all the above, said to you by people who never dream that they might be giving offence. After all, suppose I said to a doctor or a teacher: 'Oh yes, I'd like to heal/educate people if only I had the time.' Or: 'Have you ever thought of being a real doctor (or teacher)?'

See what I mean?

So if you're going to 'come out' as a romantic novelist, expect a bit of flak. But expect also a lot of happy readers. Because, yes, people do read romantic novels. Millions of people, worldwide. The book sales and library borrowing figures prove it. And some of them write letters of appreciation, telling you exactly why they like your books.

That's one of the rewards. And the others? A satisfying career (I'm not talking hobby-writing here), the flexibility of working at home as your own boss (provided you can apply the self-discipline that goes with it), and – yes, romantic novelists have to eat too – money. How much varies enormously, from the one-off payment of two or three hundred pounds offered by some publishers to the huge advance running into six or seven figures that we read of being paid to a very, very few authors. Don't expect that – but don't lose hope. It just could happen to you...

I know of no life more satisfying than that of being a writer. It is what I have wanted ever since I was five years old and first asked how stories came about. Since I began writing seriously, in my early thirties, I have developed and grown in ways I should have thought far beyond me. The idea of a book on the shelves with my name printed on the cover seemed then to be no more than a wild dream.

Yet now I have over 50 – under three different names, it's true, but *I* know that I've written them all. I've achieved that early ambition to be an 'author', but I don't think I will ever lose the desire to write something better, something new. To reach for other dreams.

I hope this book helps you to achieve your own personal ambition, whether it is to turn out a new Mills & Boon romance every month or to write one long 'doorstop' saga in two years.

I look forward to seeing your books on the shelves.

# 1
# ROMANCE – OR ROMANTIC NOVEL?

First, let's look at the difference between a romantic novel and a straight romance.

## The qualities of romance

As I see it, a romance is just that – the story of a love affair developing between a man and a woman, from the moment when they first experience that *frisson* of chemistry to the culmination of their love – whether it's a proposal, their first lovemaking, the wedding itself or even the arrival of their first baby, which has been a popular ending just recently. Any other issues are secondary and part of the background – for instance, a Mills & Boon novel might well address the issues of conservation or business ethics as part of the plot, but the real stake is in whether the hero and heroine are ever going to make up their differences and get together. Forget that at your peril.

In some ways 'romance' is an unfortunate term, conjuring up visions of pink chiffon and couples wandering off dreamily, hand in hand, into the sunset, ready to live happily ever after. The Cinderella of the fairy-tale, blissfully in love with her Prince Charming, the Sleeping Beauty awakened with a kiss.

In other words, a fantasy – but what's wrong with that? If the boys can have their science fantasy (which a lot of girls read too), why shouldn't the girls have their romance (which is by no means an entirely female province)? We all know dragons don't sing and fly around in Space – well, we *think* we know that – and we know lovers don't live happily ever after. Cinderella and the Sleeping Beauty were making rash and ill-considered decisions that none of us would advise our daughters to take – and as for sending our sons down to the local shoe-shop to find a wife... Yet the stories continue to attract. There is something in them that we enjoy, perhaps even need. Perhaps, at some deep unconscious level they tell us something; perhaps they are no more than a little 'holiday' taken from reality.

I have always found it strange that romances attract so much criticism, while the James Bond type of fantasy is held up as something to admire. What is it about casual sex and violence that is so much more commendable than the boy-meets-girl story that is the basis of a romance, with its portrayal of two people struggling towards understanding?

Isn't romance, in fact, far more likely to be the experience – a looked-for expected, *wanted* experience – of most people at some time during their lives than the far-fetched series of chases, murders and beautiful, half-dressed, willing women of the spy thriller?

Well, all right, so there's a lot going for the shaken but not stirred Bond, but there's just as much, if not more, to be said for the hero of the romance, who is very much stirred by the heroine and, therefore, by the reader who identifies so strongly with that heroine and so should find it easy to fall in love herself with the strong, masculine figure at the heart of the story. And believe – for just a little while – that he is in love with her.

These are the essential ingredients of the romance. A heroine who can be identified with, and emotion that comes straight off the page and into the heart of the reader. Not fantasy after all – just the everyday experience we all look for and expect. But without these, the story itself will have no heart, and without heart there can be no romance.

Let's just have a look at that word 'romance'.

The thesaurus on my computer defines it thus:

1. affair, amour, attachment, intrigue, liaison, passion, relationship. 2. charm, colour, excitement, fascination, glamour, mystery, sentiment. 3. fantasy, fiction, idyll, legend, melodrama, novel, story, tale.

The dictionary is slightly more dismissive:

love affair; mysterious or exciting quality; novel or film dealing with love, especially sentimentally; story with scenes remote from ordinary life.

I am inclined to dispute those assumptions about 'ordinary life'.

I have written some 50-odd novels, all of which have a romantic theme or thread running through them and a number of which are purely romances. And although my heroines find themselves in all kinds of interesting and exciting situations, I don't think there is one that could not possibly happen to today's 'ordinary' girls. Many, indeed, have been written from my own experience or the experiences of other 'ordinary' people.

Exotic locations such as Iceland or the Grand Canyon can be visited by anyone who cares to save up the money for the fare. Ballooning, skiing, snorkelling and diving can be enjoyed by women and men from all walks of life. And almost every one of us either has known or will experience the delights of blossoming romance, courtship, and sexual fulfilment at some point in our lives. There is nothing 'remote' about that. It is in itself 'ordinary'. It just doesn't feel like it when it happens.

The writer of romantic stories does nothing more than conjure up the heady emotions of those days when love first begins to bloom. Remember them? Those days that seemed all sunshine, when you walked down streets never normally on your route, because there was a chance of meeting the loved one? Those nights filled with stars, when you wandered hand-in-hand, wondering if tonight would be the night he kissed you? The scent of roses, which even today can bring back the tremulous desire that swept over you the first time he dared to slip his arm around your shoulders? The taste of wine on his lips the first night you made love...

And if you are a man, you will share those memories. Romance is not the sole province of the female. You were there too – it wouldn't have been much of a romance if you weren't – and you were the other one wandering hand-in-hand, casually strolling off your normal route, smelling those roses. *You* were the one who did the arm-slipping and the kissing, remember?

Even if the image is less moonlight-and-roses, even if young love blossomed in the back of a car, and the heady nostalgia of romance is brought back by the smell of petrol or the taste of a burger and chips, the emotion remains the same, and the task of the writer does not change. The young girl who has not yet experienced love wants to know what it *will* feel like, wants to know that the unfamiliar sensations she is experiencing are normal. The older woman wants to relive them, to know that she is still capable of an emotion that reminds her of her youth.

Neither, despite the fears of the feminists, is giving way to fantasy. The girl will happily put down her book and go off with the boy next door – even if he is a skinhead and dressed in black leather – to enjoy her own special brand of romance. And the woman will set about getting a meal ready for her husband quite as cheerfully, even if he is short and balding and had all his teeth out yesterday.

And I am not just talking stereotypes. These days, the woman may be the one coming home to a meal cooked by her husband. The girl might be training to be a policewoman or a stockbroker. But we are all the same under the skin, we all want and need love, and before love can grow we need 'romance'. It is a necessary stage.

And the happy ending that is so much decried by the 'realists'? Well, let me be bold and come right out with it. There is nothing wrong with a 'happy ending' – provided you do not imply that they will live 'happily ever after'. That *is* the stuff of fairy-tales. And I note that nobody has ever actually mentioned what happened to Cinderella after the wedding, or to Sleeping Beauty when she has been awakened with that kiss. Who knows what kind of husband Charming made, and would the young man who fought his way through all those thorns have turned out to be the kind of husband who goes off to cross the polar ice-caps or live in a tent at the top of Mount Everest? Undoubtedly glamorous, but probably hell to live with, if you can pin him down long enough to find out!

What a romance does is describe the *progress of the love story*, from meeting to that moment that we all reach when we decide to commit ourselves to another person. At that point, we all – unless we are entering into such an arrangement very cynically – *expect* to live reasonably happily ever after. Whether we do or not is another story – the straight novel, if you like, after the romance. But we have the expectation and so do the protagonists of a romance. *And that is all.*

No promises are made, and the reader can make up her own mind – if she wants to – as to how the story would proceed.

But if the author has done the job properly, we will have every hope for the best. And along the way, we have enjoyed and identified with emotions that are wholly human, emotions almost every one of us will experience. If the relationship seems likely to succeed – as it should, for the writing of any other kind of story under the guise of a romance would in itself be a cynical act – then we will put the book down feeling relaxed and comforted.

And that is all I believe a romance should do. It should not hold out false expectations, nor make promises that can't be redeemed. It should simply tell a story of two people who fall in love, who encounter and overcome obstacles to that love, and who stand at last together to face life as we all must face it – but with each other's strength and support to rely on along the way.

But perhaps not quite all. That is indeed the core of a romance – *inner conflict*. The rest of it is another story – the plot, the outer conflict, packed with incidents and scenes that develop throughout the book, building up to the cliff-hangers at the end of each chapter, carrying us forward into the next, holding our attention to the very end when both inner and outer conflicts are resolved in a satisfying – we might almost say *orgasmic* – climax.

## The romantic novel

A romantic novel can range wider. In deference to its title (SOED: *novel: a fictitious prose narrative in which characters and actions representative of real life are portrayed in a plot of more or less complexity*) it can and should be rather more realistic than the 'fantasy' of pure romance. The romantic novel takes in the seamier side of life, the grit and the toughness, the unfairness, the tribulations and hardships and sheer bad luck that many people have to face. At the same time, it should not be downbeat. There should always be a thread of hope, an optimism, that while some of the characters (and not just the 'baddies') do undoubtedly suffer, our heroes and heroines will eventually come up smiling. Smiling rather wryly, perhaps, and having learned that few of us ever lead charmed lives, but able to look forward to a resolution of their problems and a better life hereafter.

Margaret Graham (author of *A Distant Dream, A Bitter Legacy*, etc.) believes that romantic novels extend the 'romantic' quality of a book whilst still giving the reader the emotional satisfaction of love in its many forms. 'These novels,' she says, 'discuss love between real people and are increasingly about values and lifestyle, and are frequently set in a very specific and active social and even political context.'

The romance's quality of fantasy comes from the fact that the seamier side of life is simply left out. It doesn't come into such stories. To include it takes a story out of the realm of 'romance' and brings it into a different category. And whereas there is nothing in a romance that couldn't happen in real life, there is a lot that happens in real life that doesn't get portrayed in a romance. Perhaps that is what its critics object to in it.

But in a romantic novel, there is no such bar. Let's have another look at that dictionary – and here it is the definition as applied to music that I find most appropriate: *characterised by the subordination of form to theme, and by imagination and passion*. Now, isn't that exactly what we are doing when we write a novel? Doesn't *theme* rise above mere *form*? And aren't *imagination* and *passion* the two most vital ingredients?

So, what do we have when we put the two definitions together – *a story of imagination and passion, with a theme in which real characters live real lives, with a plot that may be simplicity itself or as complex as* War and Peace. And *there's* a romantic novel, if ever there was one.

Doesn't the very definition excite you? Doesn't it make you want to put down this book and rush off to your word processor this very minute? I can tell you, I'm having a hard time staying with this task.

Scottish author Margaret Thomson Davis (author of *The Breadmakers Saga, Rag Woman, Rich Woman*, etc.) believes a writer must have imagination too. 'A very special kind of imagination, and not only in dramatic intensity. It is tied up with another important part of a writer's equipment: an insatiable curiosity about people. Imagination, the ability to find out how others live or would want to live is, I believe, the basis of literature.'

Romantic novels, then, are warm, emotional stories that give you a good feeling – the sort of stories that won't send you away thinking how dreadful the world is.

There are plenty of 'straight' novels that will make you think, that will enlighten you and help you to understand the 'human condition' (such as it is). But there are also times when you don't want to be informed or depressed. Times when you want to relax, to be entertained, to be told a story, as you were when you were a child, to drift away pleasurably into a world of make-believe where you can be safe in the knowledge that nothing disturbingly terrible is going to happen to the characters with whom you are – willingly – involving yourself. They may meet what seem to be insurmountable obstacles, they may suffer disappointment and conflict, even heartbreak, but *you* know – because this is a romantic novel – that all will be well in the end. The obstacles will be overcome, the conflict resolved and the disappoint-ment outweighed by the joy. That is what is meant, in this context, by 'romance'.

Being human, we also associate romance with love, and the sexual relationship that is enjoyed within love, and we expect these ingredients in a romantic novel. For true romance, there must be love, or at least the promise of it, rather than sexual gratification. This is what puts romantic novels into the 'women's writing' genre – even though many men also enjoy the romantic novel, and even though the author (who may actually be a man) isn't consciously writing for women alone.

To my mind, this perception is unfortunate but a fact of life. It may change; but in the meantime, the best thing to do is just keep on writing what we want to write and let our reader's vote with their feet, their purses and their library tickets.

## Summary

- Never forget that romance is the heart of the story.
- A romantic novel is a story of passion and imagination.
- Forget the criticism and just keep writing.

# 2
# CHARACTERS ARE PEOPLE

## Creating characters

> Characters are the linchpin of your book. Without
> characters, there is no story.

There is no mystique about characters, no magic formula. The days of
the tall, dark and handsome hero and the sweet, elfin-faced heroine
have gone. These days, we have human beings. Just like you and me
– whatever you and I are like. I know what I'm like, but I don't know
much about you. Are you the gingham-frocked Doris Day next door,
the tawny, romping Jilly Cooper, the sexy Madonna or the frankly
large Dawn French? All human beings, all quite capable of being a
heroine in a romantic novel.

What they do have in common, these ladies, is a sense of self-esteem.
They respect themselves and they don't apologise for what they are. If
they haven't been to assertion classes they probably don't need to.
They're feisty, lively, interesting. The days of the vapid, self-depre-
cating little shrinking violet are over – and a good thing too.

Feminists often disparage the romantic novel for providing a bad role
model for young girls to follow. Yet take a quick look at some of my own
heroines: TV director, ace skier, interior decorator, journalist,
managing director of a glass factory – not exactly crushed, submissive
'little women'. And because they are strong women, their stories have
to be strong too. They simply wouldn't be fazed by the old-fashioned
does-he, doesn't-he dilemma.

This doesn't mean they don't have faults. We can see our heroine making real mistakes – an ill-suited marriage, a quarrel that leads to a family feud, a wrong decision. She can be headstrong, wilful, selfish and sexy – think of some of the great heroines of past romantic novels: Moll Flanders, Becky Sharpe, Scarlett O'Hara. Need I say more?

Katie Flynn (author of *Rainbow's End*, *A Liverpool Lass*, etc.) warns against taking this too far: 'Don't choose a heroine who is in no way loveable or who acts in a manner that makes a mockery of the average reader's values. Heroes must be strong but they should never be brutal or totally unfeeling; if they act nastily, give them a reason for such actions.'

Faults should be 'positive' – traits that make a character vibrant and interesting, the kind of thing with which a reader can identify without feeling guilty. And it is with these traits that you can develop your character – they are the ones that will drive the story along, keeping the reader hooked, and it is these that you can develop to allow your heroine to mature during the story, or overcome the obstacles she will meet.

But how do we create such characters? Larger than life, perhaps, yet warmly human, living life to the full and giving our readers a sense of sharing that life with them. Do we have to be such characters ourselves? How can I, a pretty ordinary woman, or you – who may or may not be just as ordinary – create someone who will grab the imagination and live down the years as Moll Flanders or Scarlett O'Hara have done?

Well, I'm no Moll Flanders, nor a Scarlett O'Hara, but I've had quite a number of 'life' experiences just the same. Marriage, children, divorce, remarriage, stepchildren, bereavement, love, laughter, worry, fear, tears... all these have come my way, just as many or all of them will also have come yours. They are the stuff of life and the stuff of fiction. They add up to experience.

And not just experience. If you are a writer – and I include all those who may not yet be published, but will be someday – you will be adding observation of both your own experience and that of others. You will be evaluating it, considering it, applying your own insight. You might not be doing it consciously but if you are a real writer, you'll be doing it all right. In fact, many writers feel a vague sense of shame that, even during their most painful sufferings, they are suddenly aware of a little figure sitting on their shoulder with a notepad, muttering: 'This is what it feels like to be...' Feel ashamed if you must. But also feel grateful, for this little notetaker is an essential part of a writer's equipment and the notes will be there for you to draw on later.

You don't have to have experienced everything you describe in your books. The notetaker is only a part of you. But the experiences you have had will have helped make you the person you are. And it is the writer in you who will add understanding, insight and imagination, so that you will be able to understand how your characters are feeling, and interpret those feelings by translating them into words for your reader to understand as well.

Patricia Burns (author of *The Trinidad Street Trilogy*, *The Packards*, etc.) advocates actually looking for experience. 'Never turn down the chance to experience something new,' she says. 'From rock climbing to belly dancing to running a stall at a boot fair, everything can be useful. And the same applies to your emotional life. Store up those moments of sheer happiness, of frustration, of bewilderment, to bring authenticity to your characters' feelings. Even misery and betrayal have their uses – if you have suffered, you'll know how it is for your people.'

'People' is how Marcia Willet (author of *Those Who Serve*, *The Courtyard*, etc.), who also writes as Willa Marsh, sees her characters. 'For me,' she says, 'the people come first. I don't think of them as "characters". They are real people. I see them distantly at first but, as they move closer, they bring with them their whole world: their landscape, where they live and work, what they eat and drink, what they wear and read. By the time I begin to write, they are as well-known to me as my closest friends. I can hear their voices, become aware of their idiosyncrasies; they not only drive the plot, they inhabit my life.'

There are a number of ways to create characters. Some of them do start from a stereotype – if you are writing pure romance, the character is half set up for you before you start. The reader has certain expectations. You know that you need a hero and a heroine, who are going to become involved in a story that will end in their acknowledging their love for each other. They will both be physically attractive (this is fantasy, remember!) yet human as well. They may well have flaws or hang-ups that will get in the way of their love and which they will have to overcome, and it is satisfying if these flaws dovetail, so that true misunderstandings (rather than contrived ones) can occur.

And they will have background lives. It is the development of these background lives that will help your characters come to life. I have often advocated writing a potted biography of your characters – where they grew up and went to school, what kind of family they come from, did they go to church, where they went for holidays, etc. Just answering these questions from 'out of the air' begins to build up a picture.

Another way is to conduct an 'interview' – the kind of short and snappy column popular in magazines. 'Where are you happiest?' 'What makes you angry?' 'Who would you like to share a meal with?' And so on.

Before you know it, a person is taking shape in your mind – a living, breathing person with opinions and experiences of her own. A person who is already strong enough to resist any efforts you may make to squeeze them into places they don't want to go.

If you already have a situation in mind for your story, you must consider how it will shape your character. What kind of girl wants to be a nurse, and how is she different from one who wants to be a doctor? How will having been orphaned at the age of six affect a man as he tries to form relationships? Is a champion skier essentially different from a businessman? Probably not, in that both must be determined and persevering, but what they experienced on their way to the top must have had different effects.

Look at the way in which a character arrives at the point where the book begins. They don't spring to life ready-made, at the age of twenty-four, with a full set of brand-new, shiny characteristics bought out of a catalogue. Go back to the potted biography or interview to find out what happened to them before – the 'back-story'. The more you do it, the more real they will become. And if they are real to you, they will be real to the reader.

Minor characters also need attention. You might not want to go quite so deeply into their past lives, but you still need to know them in outline. And although this might seem a chore, I promise you that all your efforts will be paid off. Just don't get so interested in them that they take over from the main characters. And if they do threaten to do so, either rethink the whole book or cut them out – yes, *right out* – and give them a book of their own.

I shall be talking later about plots, but it cannot be stressed too often that *plot comes from character*. It is what we do in life that creates our own life stories, and it is what our characters do that creates their stories. And what we do comes directly from the kind of people we are.

Writing is very like acting. A good actress will take a lot of trouble to get to know the character she is portraying. She will imagine herself into the skin of the character, try to think her thoughts, feel her emotions. That's what you must do – imagine yourself as the character, so that you know from the inside what he or she will think, feel, behave. But the actress only has to do it for one character in a story – you have to do it for every one. If you are showing a conversation between two people, you have to be both those people – giving each one equal attention. You are constantly changing skins.

That's why it is so important to *know* your characters. If you know them well enough, so well that you actually become them, you will write them with integrity. You will be unable to manipulate them into behaving in a way that is 'convenient' for the story; if you try, you'll feel uncomfortable and the story will start to go wrong.

Look on your characters like children. You might be able to guide them in their early stages, but right from the beginning they will have their own personalities and their own ways of doing things. As parents, however hard we try to make sure our children have only the 'right' experiences (whatever they may be) we really have very little control over all the influences touching their lives. By the time they are six years old, they are definitely formed as characters, and in their teens, even though you have lived with them all these years, you still can't predict exactly what they'll do. Can you write the script for your own family when they come in this evening? No – and neither should you try to do so for the characters in your book.

This may have you tearing your hair out in despair. 'But I've got to be able to write their script! I've worked out the story!' Yes, I know. And you want it to end in a certain way. Indeed, if you are writing romance, it *must* end in that way. How can you let these recalcitrant characters go wandering off on their own, trailing you miserably behind like an inexperienced reporter sent out to follow a film or television personality?

I can only say that this is part of the mystery of story-telling. Somehow or other, it does come together. There is a part of the brain, not yet identified by researchers, which will take your mixture of characters, plot, storyline, even length and style, and stir them all together and come out with something that is roughly what you want.

I say 'roughly'. Every now and then someone will surprise you by saying or doing something you hadn't anticipated, and you will have to stop and think. You might decide that this really won't do, in which case you will have to go back – not just a sentence or two, but sometimes quite a long way – and 'unpick' what you have already written. But often you will see that this is actually a better way to let the story develop and, even if it means rethinking your lovely plot, you will go along with it. There is no reason why that plot, worked out weeks or even months ago, has to be set in stone; no reason why you shouldn't, as you get deeper into the story and grow to know your characters more thoroughly, have a better idea.

## Naming characters

One of the most important aspects of a character is his or her name. A name can make or mar the impression you want to give your reader.

As Leslie Dunkling (name expert and author of *The Guinness Book of Names*, *Our Secret Names* and others) points out, there is a central stock of names that have been used through many centuries and are as familiar to us today as they were in the Middle Ages – John, Mary, Elizabeth, Matthew, etc. These retain a fairly constant popularity. Then there are less well-known but equally ancient names like Osmund, Avis, Beulah, Everard. Finally, there are 'new' names like Tracey, Wayne, Ryan or Zara.

Think of any of these names and you will probably have an instant picture of its owner. John – steady, dependable. Zara – lively, exotic. What's more – and this is the important point – in most cases, your impressions will be very similar to mine. This is because we have all heard these names in roughly the same degree and applied to roughly the same people. This applies more now than ever before, because of the preponderance of names we come across each day in newspapers, on TV and radio, in books and magazines. And because John is generally seen as reliable and steady, so the name will be used for that kind of character.

Not only that, parents who want a steady, reliable son will unconsciously choose that kind of name for their baby. They'll probably be steady, dependable people themselves and not likely to break out with something unusual like Beulah or Lancelot.

Now, the baby John, with such parents and such expectations of him coming from almost everyone he meets, is more likely than not to grow up in just that way – steady, dependable, predictable. Not always, of course – there will always be the exception. But childhood influences, parental expectations and social pressures have great effect, and in fiction you will find that to give a character a name that seems 'wrong' in the reader's perception will be a disaster. (And the exception might well choose to be known by a variation on his name – Johnny, or Jack.)

Names can also date a character. There are fashions in names as in everything else, and names that were popular half a century ago seem old-fashioned now. If you give your heroine's five-year-old daughter a name like Mabel, which is today more applicable to an eighty-year-old, the reader will be constantly having to adjust her ideas of this character. Every time she reads the name, there will be that moment of surprise. And the name will never ring true.

Some 'new' names can suffer from a bad press. Tracey and Sharon, both nice enough names, have taken a terrible battering and are probably hardly used in fiction now. Even using them for the stereotypes they represent would be a cliché. So anyone who used them in books before they gained their unfortunate present-day connotations will find that the image they originally wanted to present has been distorted.

From this, we can learn not to be too eager to use newly popular names. If you want something unusual, it might be better to go to older stock, such as Biblical names, many of which are gaining in popularity – Joshua, Benjamin, Daniel, Ruth, Esther. Always think of the parents – what kind of people they were, and what kind of name they would favour.

Some people, and these will invariably be those who are themselves more flamboyant personalities, choose to give their children much more unusual names, perhaps something they have read in a book or even made up themselves. This can be carried to extraordinary lengths and I can't help wondering what little Peaches and Cream or Fifi Trixiebelle are going to do when they grow up. Don't these parents *love* their children? But perhaps children born to parents who take so little account of social pressure will (a) inherit that insouciance and (b) get so used to it that they don't even realise their name is out of the ordinary.

The important point for you as a fiction writer is that *you* take account of all these factors and choose your names according to your characters' (and their parents') personalities.

## Describing your characters

So far I have not mentioned physical description of your characters. I find that I use this in less and less detail, and have noticed that other novelists tend to do the same. In pure romance, it does still seem to be an important ingredient, but unfortunately there are only a few eye colours, and not many more in hair and a limit to the ways in which these can be described. And quite a lot of readers actually prefer not to have descriptions imposed on their own imagined characters.

However, if you do want to describe your characters, there are a few rules that must be observed.

Describe your character as early as possible, so that your reader can start to build the picture you want her to see. In a romance, description of characters and background is important. The reader wants a picture painted. She wants to know what the characters look like, and she wants this picture painted throughout the book. But just giving the heroine tawny hair and green eyes isn't enough. You need several other ways of describing her hair and eye colour. You don't need to mention them on every page, but you do need the occasional reminder where it can add to the characterisation or the action.

Some publishers of romance, particularly Mills & Boon, also like clothes to be described. This can be tricky, as too way-out fashions can date a book, and even though the book will only be sold in the shops for a few weeks, it may remain on library shelves for years. So, unless your heroine is a fashion designer or model, keep clothes reasonably classic. Some styles of dress are almost always around, and items like jeans go on for ever. Use colour – also giving you an opportunity to remind us about hair colour, figure, etc – but please, *please* – just for me – avoid that fashion-page cliché 'teaming'. Does anyone really 'team' a navy sweater with white slacks?

Don't describe your character from head to toe all at once. Pick on the most arresting feature first – height, hair, eyes, smile – and bring in the others gradually. If you give her actions or gestures as she speaks, you can enliven her dialogue as well as bring in another nugget of description – waving her long, slender hands as she speaks, for instance, or tossing back her blonde hair. Don't use those. They're rotten even for clichés. But you get the drift.

## Using body language

The best kind of description tells you something about the character as a person, rather than just what he or she looks like. The way a man walks or stands, the way a woman uses her eyes or arranges her body in a chair. These are the clues we look for, often unconsciously, in assessing a person when we meet them for the first time. And even though a lot of the information we take in is unconscious, the reader will still recognise it (on the same unconscious level) if you use it in your narrative. You don't have to *say* that when Jake folded his arms across his chest it was a gesture of rejection. The reader will recognise it as one, without even realising she's done so. She'll 'just know' what Jake is doing and what the other character, the rejected one, is feeling, just as she knows it when it happens in real life.

Body language gives action to what might otherwise be a static scene, adds a picture, deepens insight into your characters. Without it, you get one of those long strings of dialogue, often without even a 'he said' to break it up and remind you who's talking. And while the dialogue itself should also tell you something about the speakers, such a presentation seems to me to be a missed opportunity to enrich the whole story.

# Summary

- Let your characters be human – remember they're *people*.

- Use your own experience and insight.

- Choose the right names for your characters.

- Describe your characters early.

- Use body language to express emotion.

# 3

# CHARACTERS TALKING

## Dialogue

Dialogue seems to bother a good many writers. It can seem very stilted if you don't get it just right. Yet if you try to reproduce it exactly as people speak, it can be anything from verbose to silly.

Well, the good news is that there is more to help us today in the writing of dialogue than there has ever been before. Examples of different speech patterns are around us all the time – and if we don't have time to listen to them right now, we can even save them for later and listen over and over again until we can reproduce them accurately inside our own heads.

Radio and TV are a boon. Every day there are plays, soaps, documentaries, phone-ins, films and even game shows that provide a rich seam of speech to listen to. And a lot of it is authentic, not acted.

Other such sources are audio books. The tape-recorded novels of, say, Catherine Cookson will give you a good sense of the speech patterns of the north-east. D. H. Lawrence will help out with Nottingham, Winston Graham's *Poldark* novels with Cornwall... And it's no chore to listen to any of these.

Many local libraries have an oral history section, where local people, mostly elderly, talk about their memories. The history itself can be useful too, though you need to remember that memories can distort reality. The speech patterns, however, will be authentic.

Take every opportunity of listening to people talking – on a train, in a pub or cafe, at a party, wherever you can. And it's best if you can just listen to someone else's conversation, rather than join in. (A great excuse to eavesdrop.) Then you can hear two people – maybe more – interacting. Listen to the way they use words, the cadences and patterns of speech – these are far more important than any quaint spelling. Even people who speak 'received English' and believe they have no accent will have their own little idiosyncrasies that will be recognised and enjoyed by the reader. Take note of the ways they emphasise their points – either physically, with body language, or by using tricks of speech, particular inflexions or the repetition of certain words.

Try to hear your characters' voices in your head, to *think* with a Welsh lilt or an American twang. When you write it down, you may not see much difference in the words on the page, but your reader can pick up on it and read it in the same accent. It will work for her. And if it's an accent she's never heard, no amount of dropped h's and quaint spelling will bring it to life for her. It's best not to try.

Dialect is largely a matter of different grammatical construction and word order, mixed up with words and phrases that are peculiar to a particular locality. People say it is dying out now – and with so much movement of population, so that fewer people stay in the area where they grew up, it probably is – but you can still hear broad Devonshire or Lancashire spoken in the appropriate places. Don't confuse it with accent, and take care with words and phrases that may be clichés and inaccurate – 'boyo' and 'bach' aren't used all over Wales, but I do know a Glaswegian who often uses the phrase 'right enough' and even says 'Och' and 'wee lassie'.

Apart from the sprinkling of a few dialect words, it is the pattern of speech and the inflexion that is generally more effective in writing. And you can use these to great effect. An otherwise commonplace police sergeant was brought hilariously to life in a crime novel I read recently by the author's giving him the habit of lifting his voice at the end of each sentence, so that every statement sounded like a question. His few short appearances, which would have been necessary but dull, were thus transformed, all with the use of a single punctuation mark.

Don't make all your characters use the same expressions. One man will say 'Blimey!' and another 'Jesus!' or 'Heavens above!' But every character in a book won't use the same exclamation – they'll each have a favourite. This helps, too, in identifying which character is speaking, and gives a tiny insight into that character.

Don't bother with a lot of funny spellings, I just use a few, and only for minor characters. If your main character is a Cockney it is irritating for the reader to have to grapple with dropped h's and g's as well as a lot of ain'ts and ohmygawds. There would be far too many of them. Remember that most of your readers also listen to radio plays, watch soaps and hear the same variety of speech patterns as you do, so a hint is all that is needed to let them know. Try using mangled vowels or dropped consonants once or twice when your character first speaks then unobtrusively forget them. But keep the patterns. These are what convey the flavour of speech.

Words that are peculiar to an area or way of life will add authenticity to your dialogue. But don't use them in a way that will baffle your reader, and do steer clear of too much jargon. Slang, too, can be a trap. It will often give an authentic flavour to regional or historical writing, but you need to be very careful to get the period right and not to overdo it. RAF 'types' (itself outdated slang) might have peppered their conversation with 'wizard' and 'prang' during the 1940s, but it will be as irritating to read today as sorting out all those tadpoles that scatter over a page full of dropped h's.

Probably the greatest user of slang – which was called 'cant' in the period of which she was writing – was Georgette Heyer. At her best, she gave her books a wonderful period flavour; at worst, it was unreadable. (And I have heard it said, though I don't know if it's true, that she made a lot of it up! After all, who is going to contradict her?)

You can find historical slang in the *Penguin Dictionary of Historical Slang*. It's wonderful for browsing, but to me it's the wrong way round – you have to know the slang word before looking it up. I need some kind of psychic book that will know when I want a piece of slang and tell me about it! But until some bright whiz-kid comes up with a program I can install on my computer, which will be constantly on the alert for such passages, I shall have to do what I am advising you to do: listen to people talking. There can't really be any substitute for that.

## Conversation

Let's make a couple of definitions here. Obviously, dialogue and conversation are the same thing – or are they? For writing purposes, no. Dialogue is the talk that goes on between characters – but it is there for a purpose. It drives the story along. It illuminates character, it tells us what is happening – or has happened, in the past or 'off-stage' – it enables the characters to speak their thoughts, to describe events in their own words and from their own point of view. Every word of your dialogue should serve a purpose. In every spoken exchange, there should be some nugget of information that in some way adds to the story itself.

Conversation, on the other hand, does little or none of this. Sometimes, usually midway through a book, you will find two characters engaging in friendly banter or small-talk that does absolutely nothing for the story. The purpose seems to be to show that they have (usually temporarily) overcome their differences and are now happy together. But the effect is static. The jokes fall flat. And this is because the story itself is *at the same point at the end of the exchange as it was at the beginning.*

The result is that the book sags. The storyline is the essential thread on which the book hangs, and if it is allowed to hang loose the reader's interest flags with it. The storyline must be kept taut all the time, with changes and developments taking place throughout, even if they are sometimes only tiny. There must be development, or progress, on every page.

This can make it seem difficult when you want to show, for instance, a dinner party or family meal in progress. But it isn't really. Such occasions are very useful for portraying the interactions between a group of people – with all their gestures and mannerisms, of course – and for getting across some useful or vital information or development. But if there is no such development, then they must be left out.

If it is important that we know about the dinner party, it can just be referred to as having taken place off-stage. You can do this even if something vital did happen, if it was only a small thing and describing the party would be too laborious. Just have two characters discuss it later, conveying the information during *their* conversation.

If you feel you must show the dinner party, you don't have to show it all. Keep the dialogue going just as long as is necessary to convey the information, or show the event that you want to show, with just enough atmosphere included to prevent its being too cursory. Leave the rest out – the reader will understand that more conversation did take place.

Notice how these things are dealt with on TV or in radio plays. A short scene tells us all we need to know. And that's not a bad yardstick to use. Ask yourself at intervals: does the reader need to know or see this? Does it help the story? If not, cut it out, however poetic or lyrical your prose may be.

There is, however, always the exception. Sometimes what appears to be mere desultory conversation, used skilfully, will convey exactly the information or the flavour that you want, without appearing to show any development at all in the story.

A brilliant example of this occurs in Daphne du Maurier's *Rebecca*. At a very tense point in the story, the de Winters sit down to lunch with the local magistrate and the farm manager. For a full seven pages, the four of them make stilted small talk, touching only occasionally on the reason for their being there. In short, awkward sentences they discuss subjects ranging from the heat in London to the extreme pippiness of raspberry jam. Yet the tension never flags; indeed, the very awkwardness of the conversation adds to the suspense because we know that in the minds of each one of them the discovery of a body is uppermost, and we are as anxious as they to know what is going to happen about it.

Later in the book, there is another episode over a meal. The narrator says that she remembers 'every detail'. She remembers what they ate, which she describes in the barest detail; she remembers the candles and the drawn curtains. *Yet that is all she describes.* She doesn't describe any conversation and the first event she mentions is the ringing of the telephone while they drink their coffee and the story begins to move forward again.

From this, we can learn that development in a story does not necessarily mean action or incident; it can mean the conveying of atmosphere, the building of suspense. 'Conversation' that does this is very difficult to achieve, but when it works it can be brilliant. But it *doesn't* work when you are portraying a scene that has no incipient suspense, or conflict. Because a story without conflict is a story without movement, a story that has stopped. And, like an old car, it can be very difficult to get it moving again.

If you find that you do have such a spot in your story, an oasis where all is peace – albeit temporarily – don't dwell on it. Mention it, refer to it, and get on with the action again. Get back to the suspense. That's what the reader wants.

## Summary

- Stories come from people – know your characters as people.

- Make dialogue work for the story.

# 4

# FROM SETTING TO STYLE

## Settings

Telling a story is such an intricately woven affair that it is impossible to say where you should start. Plot comes from character, but where do characters come from? Sometimes, you need to start with the setting for your story and work from there.

I have already suggested that a character's background will have a significant effect on the kind of person they are. This is obvious in such background influences as family, schooling and so on, but there are other factors too. One is the background of the workplace.

All of my 'Donna Baker' historical novels have been set in an industry – glassmaking, carpet-weaving, iron-mining or paper-making. From these industries came the characters and their stories. All were set in the nineteenth century, when such industries were family-run – indeed, some of them still are. Each had its own way of life, its own traditions, its own successes and problems, its own jargon. And whereas the personal problems encountered by my characters could have been those of anyone, in any business, the pressures of their working lives were theirs alone. This gave the backbone to the stories, and the characters who had grown up with these traditions and pressures were the flesh.

I also used such themes in my Mills & Boon romances. Glassmaking (again), ballooning, sculpting, journalism, TV – all made strong backgrounds against which the story took place. And the stories *depended* on those backgrounds – that's the important point. The hero and heroine in *Sky High* would never have met if they hadn't both been balloonists; Tim and Cordelia (in *Chalice*) would never have gone to Corning, in America, if they hadn't been part of a glassmaking family.

Place can shape characters too. Walking in Slovenia some years ago, I was struck by the rugged toughness that I saw in the faces of the local people – a ruggedness that seemed to echo the harsh, indomitable mountains that surrounded them. This ruggedness was graphically displayed during the Second World War when Tito's partisans retreated to those very mountains and held out with grim determination against the German invaders.

Look at the difference between the characters of Jane Austen and the Brontës. In the softer climate and manicured countryside of the south, we find a very different set of characters, playing out very different stories, from those in the bleaker, more robust north.

It isn't that southerners are necessarily softer. It seems to me that, just as I noticed in Slovenia, tough countryside brings out the toughness in human beings. And their stories will be tougher as well.

Sometimes, the place where a character lives, or the work they do, may be so important to that character and to the development of the story that it has to be given special attention. It becomes almost a character in its own right.

Margaret Graham says that using what she calls an *active* setting lends depth to a novel. She suggests, for instance, having your heroine toiling in some pioneering sense alongside her partner. 'As they develop their project, how does their relationship progress? How do they progress as individuals in response to the environment? Ask yourself question after question, keeping in mind that the relationship is paramount. Everything must be relevant to its progression.'

In such a story, you will need to understand and portray that background – a way of life, an industry perhaps – in some detail. Typical of this are the many 'trouble at mill' stories of which I suppose my own 'Glassmakers' trilogy (*Crystal, Black Cameo* and *Chalice*) are examples. In a story that depends largely upon a geographical setting, such as the adventure stories of Hammond Innes, you will need to know the area well. (There are, invariably, exceptions: the Inspector Ghote stories of H. R. F. Keating were written without Keating's ever having visited Bombay. Myself, I wouldn't dare!)

My feeling is that if you use guidebooks, however good, you are using only second-hand impressions and, more important still, someone else's style. Just as in characterisation and in story-telling itself you are using your own insights, so you should be doing in your descriptions of real-life places. What you see and are struck by will be different from what your favourite travel writer saw. And since the purpose of your writing is to use *your* voice, why let someone else have a say? Moreover, because you have different interests and perceptions, you might – indeed, almost certainly will – come across something that adds vitally to your story, and which you would have missed if you had not made the effort to go and look for yourself.

I have almost invariably written only about places I have seen for myself. A rare exception is a section in *Bid Time Return* which is set in 19th-century Tibet. Since it is difficult even to visit 20th-century Tibet, I decided to break my self-imposed rule. I did a lot of research, however, and a number of people have asked me how I enjoyed the trip I must have made! So it can be done. But I still wonder what I might have added to the story if I really had been there.

Some writers excuse themselves by saying that if you are writing a historical novel you can't go back in time to see places as they were. True. But you can usually get a fair idea, because in most cases there are still a number of buildings still standing, old maps in existence, and field systems or roads recorded, which can give you a distinct feeling for the place. And the shape of the ground, the hills and valleys, and the sky are generally not much different. It still helps to stand in old streets and close your eyes and ears against today's traffic. That's what your imagination is for.

Don't, however, get so interested in your setting that it takes over from your characters and the story you are telling. I have fallen into this trap myself, and had to cut pages of flowing description that added nothing to the story. Like 'conversation', too much description can make the book static.

Even if the background plays a less vital part, it is still important in creating atmosphere. Mary Stewart attaches great importance to 'place' in her romantic suspense stories, and her feeling for it comes through in her writing. And here again is that important point, which cannot be repeated too often: you must have an interest in, better still

a passion for, what you are writing. If you hate being amongst mountains you will not be able to convey their majestic beauty with any
conviction. (But you may be able to convey the feelings you have about
their menace.)

Romances are frequently set in exotic locations, often places where
readers might go (or long to go) on holiday. They convey the same
freshness and delight that one feels when waking up in a warm, sunny
spot, perhaps with the sound of waves lapping a sandy beach. They set
the scene for the kind of story that the reader expects.

This is not to say that you can't set a romance in an industrial inner-
city. But it needs to have quite a lot else going for it. And the same
goes for cold countries. There is no reason why a romance shouldn't be
set in Iceland – where I have set one of my own stories – but warm
countries are perceived as being more romantic.

Remember that millions of romantic novels are sold to other countries,
from Poland to Japan, and to many of these Britain itself is exotic.
Scotland has long been a favourite setting for romances, and I and
others have had success with stories that take place amongst the
golden stones of the Cotswolds, the thatched villages of Devonshire or
the indisputably romantic mountains of the Lake District. Again,
choose 'holiday' settings, which foreigners will be more likely to have
heard of or want to visit. (You will also have the satisfaction of having
done your bit for the tourist industry.)

## Theme or formula?

Many hopeful authors (including myself!) have asked: What is the
formula for a romance? There is a widespread belief that when you are
'in the know' your publisher will hand you this formula – presumably
a seven-point plan with stops for kisses along the way – and fame and
fortune are on the way.

Sadly, no. There is no formula, other than that of *boy-meets-girl, boy-
loves-girl, obstacles-get-in-the-way* until finally *boy-gets-girl*. That's *it*.

But this is not a formula for success. You could probably apply that
'formula' as much to the great classical novels as to the latest Mills &

Boon romance. True, they sometimes go on to add another dimension – *boy-loses-girl* – but that basic formula is there.

It is the way you tell the story – your own, unique treatment of it – that lifts it above a mere formula. And this is partly a function of style, which we'll discuss later, and partly of structure. And very largely of the theme you are trying to express. Because plot, on its own, is not enough. And even the simplest love story must have a theme that is the purpose in telling it.

The pure romance, usually a fairly short novel of less than 200 pages, is a straightforward love story. It deals with the relationship between a man and a woman, charting their progress from a significant moment in that relationship to the moment when they finally commit themselves to each other as lovers.

My story *A Man Possessed* tells the story of a young married couple who have been working together as interior designers. Trouble comes when they begin to move in different directions careerwise, and are forced to look at their marriage to discover what is really important to them. By the end of the book, the heroine has also faced the truth about her relationship with her mother and the insecurities she has suffered from throughout her life. In short, she has grown up.

The theme of the story is possessiveness. Because she feels insecure, the young woman is trying to maintain control over both her husband and her mother. But she can't see this. To her, it is the mother who is being possessive, and her husband who is jealous. It takes quite a lot of heart-searching, and very nearly the loss of her marriage, before she is able to see what is happening and start to put things right.

In *Bid Time Return*, the theme is more complex. Here, I was interested in the way that patterns repeat themselves throughout our lives, sometimes for several generations. I wanted to use the Eastern concept of *karma* to illustrate this, while showing that it can also be attributed to such factors as upbringing and problems handed on by parents to their children. I wanted to leave the question open for the reader to ponder.

The 'Street At War' series (*Goodbye Sweetheart*, etc.) was different again. The theme was the way ordinary people on the 'Home Front' faced the hardships brought about by a war that was different from any that had gone before. In fact, I didn't have to think about this; just setting out to tell their stories was enough to develop the theme. It was too strong to be lost.

All stories need a theme; they wouldn't be satisfying stories without. But don't strive too hard to find one and drag it in. I rather believe that we all have our own pet themes lodged within us that will surface whatever we write. Perhaps that's why we write at all.

## Your voice, your style

Style is vitally important to your chances of success, yet it is something you should never worry about. I won't say you either have it or you haven't, and I won't say it can't be learnt. In as far as it is partly a matter of knowing how to use the English language, it certainly can, and must, be learnt. Not because we have to be pedantically careful about never splitting infinitives (as one successful novelist said to me: 'I wouldn't know an infinitive if I met one, let alone how not to split it!' – a remark that suggests that, in fact, even if only subconsciously, she *does* know how not to split one) but because grammar, syntax and punctuation are all such tremendously useful tools.

Writers must be able to communicate their thoughts clearly. We must tell our stories so that readers will see the pictures we want them to see. We must be able to enlist their sympathy for certain characters, and engender dislike for others. We must amuse, frighten, entertain. *Language is our only means of doing this.* Words and the way they are used, the punctuation that gives them emphasis, are our tools. Language is a vital part of a writer's equipment, and it is worth taking time to read through a few books on the subject, as well as reading the best fiction writers there are to see just how these tools can be used.

Best of all, it is completely free. We all have it at our disposal. And we've had all our lives to learn it. It astonishes me that people will spend hundreds, even thousands, of pounds on the latest technology and still produce manuscripts that display a woeful lack of understanding of their own language. How can you be a writer without a feeling for language? How can you read the countless books there are available – not just textbooks but fiction and non-fiction of all kinds – and still not grasp the basic principles of paragraphing? *Look* at how it's done.

Every book published is a manual. See how other writers achieve their effects. One of my most memorable English lessons at school was the study of Charles Reade's *The Cloister and The Hearth*. A high point of the story is a chase with Denys and a bear. We were shown how, as the chase quickens, so Reade's sentences grow shorter. Without consciously realising it, we get the impression of speed, of quickening breath, of fear. And we can't stop reading. We've got to keep on. To the end. To find out what happens next.

This is a time when you can throw some of the rules out of the window. Breaking sentences in unusual places – using tricks of punctuation such as dots or dashes – can change the tempo of the reading and bring about the impression of emotion, of hurry, of actual speed. But don't overdo such tricks. Once the reader has noticed them, they become irritating.

Clichés are like ants. They'll creep in anywhere and be running all over your story before you know it. Dianne Doubtfire, author of *The Wrong Face* and other novels, says: 'If a phrase feels familiar, it's probably because it's a cliché.' It might even be your own cliché – a phrase you've originated and used too many times. So if you get that feeling of familiarity, stop and rethink.

Don't strive for imagery. It is easy to go too far, finding a supposedly poetic image for almost everything. Comparing derelict buildings with rotten teeth may be effective the first time, but next time you've got to think of something different. Better still, just call them derelict. Such detail is quite graphic enough; it doesn't need to be dressed up all the time. And what people feel about them is more important than what they look like.

That's a part of what is called style. But the rest comes from within yourself. It is how you express yourself, and that is the part that is unique.

Someone asked me recently whether it was important for me to feel the emotions my characters were experiencing, My answer was an emphatic '*Yes!*' If I don't feel the pain or the joy, how can I expect it to come through my words and touch the reader? And yet I found it difficult to explain just how this works. I could not give my questioner a set of rules.

I think it must be because when you are emotionally involved, your use of language changes and you unconsciously pick the words and phrases that best express your own feelings. There is conscious use as well, of course – I may spend quite a long time thumbing through Roget's *Thesaurus* to hit on exactly the right word – but that's the point, it has to be *exactly the right word for me*. Only when I am satisfied that my choice of language comes as near as possible to expressing what I believe is being felt by my character at that moment can I go on with the story.

The reader has a part to play in this, as well, and it may be that my choice of words is not right for them. That can't be helped. Often enough, it is – and this may be the most important piece of advice I will give you in this book. *If your choice of language touches enough readers in the right way, if you can convey the emotions of your characters so that your reader feels those same emotions, then you are a true writer.* Much of the rest is technique, which can be learned: this is the essential part.

Don't let this dishearten you. I believe that if we want to do something badly enough, we have within us the ability to do it. Just as small children can, without having any idea what is involved, express a strong desire to learn a particular musical instrument, and go on to become masters of that instrument, so, I think, do writers know instinctively that they can write. I knew at five years old, before I could even form letters, that I wanted to become 'an author'. The story-telling instinct is a strong one, and if you have it all you need to do is find the right way for you to train and use it.

And don't forget that readers vary, and their experiences also vary. You may touch one reader with one description and another with something else. I have sometimes asked readers what it is they most enjoyed or were most touched by in my books. For instance, in *Goodbye Sweetheart*, there are a number of scenes that, in the writing, I found equally affecting. There is a scene showing young children of four or five years old setting off on evacuation, watched by their heartbroken mothers; there are scenes showing children being ill-treated by their foster-parents; there is the scene at Dunkirk as soldiers waded waist-deep into the water to be rescued.

Most people were touched by these scenes too – but not all. One man was reduced to tears at the thought of 'those poor little mites' shut in a cupboard; another found it 'faintly amusing' (and no, he's not a sadist – it may even be that he *was* touched, but found it difficult to deal with). One woman thought it was moving, but her real tears came as she read about Dunkirk. Another was almost liberated by this description, for she felt that at last she understood what her brother had endured but never been able to explain.

*What touches your readers is affected by their own experience.* So it is partly out of your hands, and you can't expect to appeal to them all. But there are many experiences that are common to us all, and you can expect to reach the majority of your readers through your description of such events *provided you feel the emotion genuinely yourself.* It *always* shows if you don't, and I believe that this is again because of our unconscious use of language. This is what reveals our own feelings, and it doesn't matter how clever you are with words, how assiduously you search the thesaurus, you will not be able to convey emotion if you do not feel it yourself. The finest prose will leave your reader cold if it is written in cold blood.

Carole Boyd, radio actress and reader of a number of novels for audio books, told me that when she came to certain parts of her reading of *Goodbye Sweetheart* she had to have a box of tissues beside her. I was surprised. Surely, I said, she would have read those passages so often beforehand that they wouldn't still have that effect on her? Certainly they would, she replied. If they didn't, she wouldn't be able to convey the emotion to the listener.

Carole understood that emotion cannot be heard unless it is there to be heard, just as it can't be read unless it is there in the writing. She was transmitting the emotion I had felt as I wrote the words, and through her own skill and tenderness it found the hearts of her listeners.

Sheila Walsh (winner of the Romantic Novelists' Association Award for Romantic Novel of the Year 1986 and author of *A Highly Respectable Marriage, Until Tommorrow*, etc.) points out: 'The first and most important ingredient of a good romantic novel must be sincerity. It should never be written tongue-in-cheek, for then it will lack the second most important ingredient, genuine emotion.'

To touch your reader with genuine emotion, you must put it on the page. It must come, in the first instance, from your own deepest feelings, and this is what we sometimes call *'writing from the heart'*.

Sheila adds: 'The characters must be real – warts and all. Very few people are all good or all bad.'

This helps to round out the story and give a feeling of reality and truth. But you can't just pop in a reference to the fact that the villain is kind to old ladies or supports the local cats' home. Whatever good traits he may have must be relevant to the plot. It is probably better to think of it as not painting him too black, rather than trying to add a few splashes of pure white.

---

# Summary

- Find an interesting setting and research it thoroughly.
- Stop looking for a formula.
- Develop your own style.
- Learn to use the English language.
- Touch your reader with the emotion *you* feel.

---

# 5
# GETTING TO WORK

## Let's write a romance

Let's look at just how you might go about writing a romance – the shortish book loved by readers of, say, Harlequin Mills & Boon – about 55–60,000 words long, with a simple plotline involving a hero and a heroine, a small number of minor characters, an attractive background and a story that is interesting enough to hold attention but will never take over from the main concern, which is the love between the two main protagonists.

In the romance, love is all. This is the archetypal boy-meets-girl. This is the book that has attracted so much criticism and 'happy-ever-after' sneers. It is also the book that sells most widely and consistently all over the world. Clearly, it is the book that women want to read more than any other, and its message must be one that women want most to hear.

And it isn't at all hard to divine just what that message is. Love *is* all. Never mind feminine subjugation, never mind liberation, in all women's hearts is the longing to enjoy a special kind of love. A love that satisfies all human instincts, that endures through life. A love you can rely on, be sure of, whatever else may happen, whatever disasters you may be called upon to face. The sort of love that we think must be enjoyed by couples who celebrate their golden weddings – even though we know they've been through fifty years' worth of ups and downs, including illness, bereavement, world wars, every sort of tragedy. But they're still together, still smiling at each other. And they'll say – I've heard them – that the happiest day of their lives was their wedding day.

That's the past seen through rose-tinted glasses. There have undoubt-edly been other days, when the world seemed to be collapsing around them and they felt that their happiness was lost. And it will be a rare couple who will be able to say truthfully that they've never wanted to hit the other over the head with something hard and heavy and generally used for frying sausages, or who have never wished they could walk away and never see the other again.

But they *are* still together. And as they look back over that fifty years, most of them do say that, notwithstanding all those ups and downs, their abiding memory is of happiness – by which, I think, they mean they have kept that thread of enduring love throughout their years and now know just how precious it is. That is the love and commitment defined in the words of the marriage service, and *that* is what is meant by 'happy ever after'. And that, I believe, is what women really want, in their deepest hearts, and what they look for in the 'romance'.

It is the flavour of the story and the tone of the writing that gives the romance its appeal. If you don't believe in this kind of love, if you distrust the opposite sex (or even your own) and dismiss marriage or the committed relationship as something that has had its day, you will not be able to write a romance. You will not have the belief or the passion that will put this message across; instead, there will be a distasteful cynicism that will leave an unpleasant flavour and create an uneasiness in the reader's mind. Even if you follow the 'formula', starting off with your heroine and hero meeting, falling in love, encountering and overcoming obstacles until at last they walk down the aisle (or, more likely these days, fall into bed), even if you describe their exotic background, her dress and blonde hair and Gucci sandals, and his taut muscles and dark, hungry looks and Rolex watch, even if you describe every smallest detail of their lovemaking and take half a chapter for every orgasm, even if you do all these things, you will still fail if you don't have that same deep belief and longing in your own heart. A simple love story, written about an ordinary, likeable girl and a truly strong hero, who don't depend on expensive trappings but have real, recognisable emotions, will succeed where yours has failed because that writer really believes in what she is writing about.

But why am I haranguing you like this? *You're* not going to write tongue in cheek, just to make a few pounds, are you? You're the one who believes in love and romance as a way to the heart, and the way to life as it should be lived. You're the one who wants to put this message across, as simply and evocatively as possible, and to as many people as you can reach in as many countries as possible. And, yes, you'd like to earn a living or at least a supplementary income while you do it.

## The nitty-gritty

The romance, as typified by Harlequin Mills & Boon (and most others of the genre follow these guidelines), is generally about 60,000 words. They are specifically 187 pages of print, but if you look at a few you will see that the size of the font will vary from book to book, or that some will have new chapters starting on new pages while others run the chapters on without a gap. This gives room for manoeuvre, so there is some margin on the word count.

The difficult thing for beginners is to work out just how much *story* is needed to fill this number of pages. If you aren't careful, you can be into the last chapter and still have half the story to tell. Or get it all over in the first six and then find yourself wondering what to do with them all for the rest of the book.

This is where structuring comes in. I have already talked about plot and structure in fairly general terms, as applied to both the romance and the broader-based romantic novel. Now let's work through a romance from scratch.

First, find your starting point. It might be a setting – somewhere fascinating and unusual where you've been on holiday, perhaps, or a particular job that you think could make an interesting background. For instance, my daughter has set up her own business (which she calls Manes 'n' Tails) as an equine beauty therapist. She pulls and plaits horses' manes and tails, prettifying them for shows, clipping them in winter, breaking in and doing all sorts of things that owners can't or don't want to do for themselves. She also takes out escorted rides on Dartmoor, where she lives.

This could be a good starting point. There are umpteen different opportunities for meeting people here. She could be called to prepare the master of hounds' own horse if his groom is taken ill – and the master, of course, would turn out to be unmarried, extremely attractive and, most important, attracted to the young woman who has come to make his horse beautiful. Note that the heroine has stopped being my daughter – she is now a character in her own right!

So we have our situation, which already looks interesting. And there is also potential for conflict. Fox-hunting is a controversial subject and not even all horsey people approve of it. There is at present a strong lobby for a complete ban. Perhaps the heroine herself feels so strongly that she has already decided not to work on hunters. She might even have taken part in demonstrations as a hunt saboteur – and encountered this very same master of hounds.

At this point, we have to find a good reason for her having to take on this particular job. Perhaps she has changed her mind over hunting. More likely, she will have some compelling need to earn the money and can't afford to be fussy over who she takes on as clients.

Why could this be? Perhaps the sick groom is a particular friend, or a member of her family, and she's doing it to help out. This could also prevent her from being too forthright with the master when he recognises her – she doesn't want to risk her friend's job. At the same time, he's going to be suspicious of her and, being a spirited girl, she's going to find it difficult to hold her tongue. Lots of potential for simmering tension there, especially when added to the smouldering attraction developing between them.

There could be other reasons why she has to take on this job. Perhaps she has her own commitments – a dependent mother, who is herself ill and needs extras that only her daughter can provide. Or she may have a child.

Heroines of romances don't have to be virgins these days. They can have been married before – perhaps widowed, but nobody can ignore the fact that there are many young divorcees now. And some are single mothers.

A young woman who has a child to support may well have to shelve some of her own principles. But that doesn't mean she has to find it easy, and her discomfort will rebound on the hero whom she may see as the villain – thus creating yet more tensions and conflicts that will have to be resolved before the story can come to its conclusion. And the more difficult that is, the better the book will be and the more the reader will enjoy it.

All this is just the start. Having created our original situation, we now need to develop the characters so that we will know how they are likely to behave in all the situations that follow – indeed, how they will create their own situations and their own story.

# The back-story

What happened in the past affects how this story begins. Suppose we decide that our heroine is a single mother, aged perhaps about 25. The child is probably under five years old. Obviously there has been a previous relationship and the story of that relationship is important. Let's call our heroine Kate. Is she a widow or divorced, or did she have a steady live-in commitment? If none of these, you may be treading on thin ice – the heroines of these romances are not promiscuous, and unlikely to have gone in for one-night stands and unsafe sex. And rape is not the subject for a romance; that belongs in a different kind of novel.

Whichever you choose, remember that it will have had an effect on the Kate we see standing in the master's yard at the beginning of the book. If she was widowed, she may still be in love with her late husband; if divorced, she may be wary and even bitter – and the ex may still be about, featuring in her life and that of her child. They'll still have feelings for each other – they may even still be half in love. It takes time to get over all the feelings involved in marriage and divorce. All this will affect Kate's dealings with life and with the men she meets – and, in particular, with the hero.

When you've got her sorted out, you've still got him to consider. Traditionally, he'll be a few years older (the toy-boy too belongs in a different kind of novel). So he's going to be at least in his thirties. What sort of relationships has he had? Has he been married? Is there a jealous ex-wife in the background, or is his house still littered with photographs from the past? Does he have any children? And how does all this affect his attitude to this uppity young woman who has tried in the past to ruin a good day's hunting and is now proposing to take a pair of clippers to his best horse?

Only when you've worked all this out, can you start to think through the story itself.

But it really isn't as hard as it may seem. All you need to do to work out a situation is ask questions. But they do have to be the right questions. Asking what colour eyes they have is no help at this stage.

The next thing to consider is what is likely to happen when these two come together. And there is, if not exactly a formula, a likely pattern of events.

## Developing the story

The opening chapters must tell the reader something about the heroine – who she is, where she is and why she's there. A thorough knowledge of the back-story is essential already – you're not going to tell the whole story to begin with, but you need to know it in order to weave it in, a little at a time. In some stories involving a child, if there has been a previous relationship the hero may actually be the father (whether he knows it or not) and you may or may not want this to become clear to the reader until later. Your choice of what you convey and the words you use are vitally important.

In these early chapters – say, the first two – you are setting the scene. But that doesn't mean a leisurely start – the action and the pace have to be there from the beginning. Both the conflict and the sizzling chemistry of attraction must be there from the very first page, the first *sentence*. Not only is this story a turning point in the heroine's whole life, the turning has begun even before she and the hero meet. She is at a crossroads. She is in desperate need. It is that need that has brought her within his sphere; without it, they might never have met.

In Kate's case, the need is to support her daughter. (Somehow, in my mind, the child has become a daughter – in yours, it may by now be a son.) Because of this, she has had to set aside her own strong feelings about hunting and probably take quite a lot of courage into her hands to go into the master's yard. (You may like to ask yourself whether or not she already knows who he is.) Probably she hopes she won't have to meet him – but of course, she does. And immediately we have the twin sparks of chemistry and conflict, setting the story into unstoppable motion.

Unstoppable? Does that mean we can just sit back and let it take its course? No, it doesn't. There's going to be many a slip before lip meets lip. And you'll find it much easier to think these through now, rather than set off on a meandering tale with no idea of how many chapters you need or will end up with, or how long to spend on any particular scene.

So picture your hero and heroine, their characters already beginning to unfold, facing each other in that stable yard. At this stage, the reader will know more about her than about him; the story is being told through her eyes, and she will already have expressed a few useful and informative thoughts about her own history – little Polly at home, just where and what 'home' is, something (but not too much yet) about how Kate comes to be in this position as a single mother, trying to run a fairly unusual business. She will also have thought a bit about her anti-hunting principles, brought to mind by her presence in this particular yard, and why she is forced to set them aside.

Already, she's in a pretty emotional frame of mind. She doesn't want to be there at all; if she meets the owner she's liable to say something she might regret, and on top of that she'll probably have some quite strong feelings about the horse she's come to deal with. She loves horses, and it isn't his fault he has to go out chasing foxes. This gives an opportunity for showing the softer side of her personality, a side the master may glimpse when he walks – sorry, *strides* – into the yard, and before she's aware of his presence.

And it's a side she may not want him to see – which will make her reaction all the sharper. Conflict is inevitable.

To outline the story from this point, you need to follow the action in your mind. How does she feel when she sees him? There will be a difference if they have indeed encountered each other before, even more if they've been involved romantically in the past. What does she do? What does she say?

It's a chain reaction. Her feelings (her hidden agenda) cause her to behave in ways that may seem entirely reasonable to her (and to the reader) but to him will seem irrational and inexplicable. So he'll react accordingly. At the same time, he too has feelings that may not yet be apparent to the reader, stemming from his own background, and these will affect his behaviour further. And that in turn will create more conflict with her...

Think it through. Pick up each link of the chain. Every event will have consequences, and the consequences will in turn lead to further developments. And all the time, the two people involved are becoming more and more closely linked by the attraction between them. The conflict will lead them to deny this, even to themselves (this is the source of the 'hating each other till the last page' syndrome) but as the attraction grows and turns into love, the denials will become more difficult to sustain.

Eventually, one – usually the heroine since she is the one the reader identifies with – will realise what has happened and admit it to herself. But she won't be able to admit it to him, because as far as she is aware he loathes her as much as she thought she loathed him. No woman is going to march up to a man who – apparently – views her with dislike and suspicion, and declare that she loves him.

Work this out against the background you have chosen. Don't forget the outward conflict – this is what's keeping them apart. At some point, we have to find a way of reconciling the two opposing view-points, and this must be a part of the story. And, equally important, we have to see the hero falling in love too. We don't see it through his eyes and thoughts, as we do with the heroine, but we must be able to detect a subtle change in his manner towards her, a hint or two that he is beginning to soften.

All this is shown through events, one leading on to another. This is what makes a story. The heroine comes to the master's yard; they have their first encounter, throwing up all kinds of conflicts, memories, problems. But she can't walk out, never to return; there must be some compelling reason why they have to meet again. This leads on to the next encounter, and so to the next. Their lives are becoming intermingled. The attraction is growing more powerful and you must find a situation in which it can overwhelm them.

This means a situation, an intimate situation, where they can be alone. As one of my Mills & Boon friends put it when I was taking my first steps, 'You have to find a way of getting their clothes off.' This could be anything from getting soaked in a sudden downpour, falling into a river, being inadvertently alone together in a bedroom when she had just stepped out of the shower, a bathroom scene, or anything more original that you can think of.

Getting their clothes off isn't really very subtle, but getting them into a situation where they can be swept into a love scene that *by this point* is not only suspected but eagerly anticipated by the reader, is essential. Predictability is dull. Will-they, won't-they suspense is exciting and page-turning. And the love scene should be both satisfying and frustrating – satisfying because the hero is clearly a fantastic lover, frustrating because for some reason the love can't at this point be fulfilled. One or other of them will draw back, or they'll be interrupted, or the outer conflict will intrude, reminding them of everything that's kept them apart up to now.

By 'love scene' I don't necessarily mean a passionate, no-holds-barred sexual encounter. That may well be what happens – until the moment of interruption – but a love scene can equally consist of little more than a kiss. It is the *emotion* that is involved that makes it a love scene, and changes the tempo of the story.

For, make no mistake, from this point the mood will change. Once such an encounter has taken place between a man and a woman, nothing will ever be the same again. And you have a number of choices, depending on the characters you have developed.

Once love has been realised, one of the participants may decide that this is more important than any principles about hunting (or whatever the conflict is) and go all out to secure happiness. You can't have both doing this, or the story would be over, so the other person must go quite the other way, deny that there is anything more than a dangerous and purely biological attraction, and fight the desire that has so inconveniently occurred. This will start off a new chain reaction and give you more events to weave into your story. Again, there can be no possibility of them just walking away into the sunset alone – they've got to be sufficiently involved to make further meetings inevitable. And the original conflict is still very much to the fore; it must be strong enough to sustain its own storyline all the way through.

Indeed, the outer conflict *has* to sustain the story and has to be resolved. Once that happens – and please don't rely on a weak resolution, like a shrugging 'oh, all right, then' – there is no bar to both being able to recognise their love and fall into each other's arms. And that's where the story ends.

This is a good, working outline, but there is not yet enough to make a story. The next step is to work it out in more detail – how they react to each other in that first meeting, what it leads to, and so on every step of the way. Write it down fairly concisely, concentrating on the essence of the events – in other words, write a synopsis. Remember that the shape of the story must be ever onward and upward – the interest content of each part must draw the reader on, so it must never sag. Everything that happens must be just that little bit more exciting or suspenseful as you go on.

## **Summary**

- Write only what you believe.
- Find a good starting-point.
- Establish your characters.
- Have a strong conflict.
- Develop your story.

# 6

# PLOTS AND STRUCTURE

## Plots

The idea for the storyline I outlined in the previous chapter came from my daughter's unusual profession. Your ideas for a romance may come from something that happens to you or to someone you know, or from something that simply occurs out of the blue. For instance, on my way to the shops one day, I suddenly wondered what might happen if a girl discovered, on her wedding day, that her new husband was still in love with someone else. This led to my novel *Last Goodbye*.

Another time, driving in the Cotswolds, my husband and I gave a lift to a young man very smartly dressed in Edwardian costume. He told us that he had been to a wedding, where everyone was requested to dress in this style. That in itself was a romantic idea. But even more interesting was his comment that the bride and groom had left the reception by hot-air balloon! This couldn't help but fire my imagination and I immediately decided that I must write a romance that ended in just this way. To make this a satisfying ending, I felt that the entire story must be closely concerned with ballooning, and before I finished *Sky High* I had learned a lot about ballooning, including spending a weekend on a course with one of the country's top balloonists (no, not that one) and enjoying a magical flight over the Cotswolds.

I don't often get ideas handed to me on a plate like that, though. Often, it is only through much hard thinking that a plot can be evolved. Frequently, I start with an industry, place or social situation and let the story come from the research. What conflicts could arise in a glassmaking factory? I asked one of the 'family' glassmakers when I was researching *The Tyzak Inheritance*, and he gave me enough material for a whole series of novels.

Later, when I wanted to use the subject for my first historical novel, I read through the history of glassmaking from early Chinese and Egyptian times until the present day, and finally decided to start with the moment in Victorian England when glassmaking was released from the crippling tax on lead. So that story was only arrived at after a lot of reading, consideration and rejection of other ideas. There had been even more dramatic moments in the history of glassmaking, but for some reason this was the one that appealed to me at that time.

My wartime quartet, written under the name Lilian Harry, came about because the publisher, Rosemary Cheetham, wanted a series of novels written about the Second World War, seen from the point of view of ordinary working-class families. I jumped at the chance. Having come from just such a family, I used my own background and the area in which I lived as a starting point and went on from there.

Most of the stories are fictional, with occasional injections from my own memory, but there is a truth that goes beyond mere anecdotal accuracy. This is the truth of what it was really like to live through those times, trying to keep ordinary family life going; how people really did behave and what their attitudes and standards were.

I believe this must be a large part of the reason for the success of these books. People have written to me from all over the world, telling me that their own memories have come flooding back. 'This was exactly what it was like to live in Portsmouth during the Blitz,' they say. And, 'I lived in that street. I remember that air raid. It was just like you say.'

My truth has touched theirs. And once again, we come back to that same vital point: you must have your own passionate interest in what you write. If you don't, that truth will not be there and your reader will be left cold.

You may think that you will never have such opportunities. But they were no more than starting points and had to be developed. Sometimes, I have to resort to other methods. It doesn't matter if they seem mechanical, as long as they fire you with that spark of passion.

Fairy stories are a good source. I suspect that all the best stories can be traced to the same basic framework as universal tales such as

*Cinderella* or *The Sleeping Beauty* – there is something deeply psychological about them. *Red Riding Hood* is a good one too. Let your heroine face a tricky situation to begin with (the dangerous forest), find herself beguiled by the 'wolf in sheep's clothing' and finally be rescued by the 'woodcutter' whose advice she rejected in the first place. And it can even be turned around, so that it is today's feisty heroine who does the rescuing!

Remember that the basis of all good story-telling is conflict. Romance itself is a form of conflict. The happy courtship and marriage with never a quiver of disturbance to its even tenor is unlikely to find many readers. (It sounds too unbelievable, for a start.) But tell the story of a heroine your reader can identify with, a hero she can fall in love with, and then put plenty of obstacles in their way, and she will stay with them to the end, increasingly anxious to see if everything turns out well.

## Sub-plots

Taking an average length of 60,000 words for a romance, an average chapter will be approximately 5,000 words. This will give you plenty of room to attend to the major development, while also permitting one or two minor developments or side issues. You may want to include a sub-plot, involving one or two minor characters – but remember that any such sub-plots must have a vital effect on the main storyline. The short romance doesn't have room for stories to run parallel.

A sub-plot is a shorter story that lies within the main story. It might involve the romance of another couple, or a different kind of story altogether – but it must be closely linked with either the hero or the heroine (or both) and its development must be crucial to the development of their love story. And it mustn't be so interesting that it overpowers them – if it's that good, it deserves its own book.

## Structure

Let's return to the bones of the story. Once you have your idea, and have worked out a storyline, your next concern is the structure – where to start, where to stop, what goes in the middle, sub-plots, flashbacks, viewpoints, and all the other traps – and opportunities – that lie waiting along the way.

I have already mentioned that you should start at a significant moment. Sometimes this is referred to as a 'crossroads' – a moment when your main character is faced with two or more choices in life. She may be starting a new job, or have just lost an old one. She may be recovering from a broken relationship, or from a bereavement.

That significant moment doesn't have to be your protagonists' first meeting, though it often is. Sometimes the story will be about two people who have known each other a long time; they may even be already married and have already lived through a previous love story (not necessarily written down) but *this* story starts at its own significant point – perhaps a change in their lives that presents a threat to their relationship, and needs to be resolved.

Any one of these could also provide you with a trigger to a new plot. What does a girl do when she's been jilted almost at the altar? How does she feel when she meets her former lover, years later, in a situation that is going to force them together – and slowly realises she still loves him?

Already the plot is beginning to unfold. But it isn't enough to have an idea that makes you sit up and reach for a pen. This is when the work begins.

The mainspring of all such stories is emotion. If the girl and her lover meet and feel nothing for each other, there is no story. But if they feel emotion – be it hate, love, a mixture of the two – then the potential for a story is there.

Charlotte Lamb (author of *In The Still of the Night*, *Walking in the Darkness*, etc.), who has written countless stories for Mills & Boon and is now making her name as a crime writer, says: 'All fiction requires some sort of tension or conflict which carries the main thrust of the novel. Conflict need not necessarily mean anger or violence – it merely implies a tension between people or ideas. The conflict of a romantic novel must be in the hero-heroine relationship – they meet, clash, are attracted, but because sexuality often makes human beings hyper-tense and edgy they are usually ready to flare up over nothing.'

The conflict here is emotional. Emotion drives us to do things, it motivates our behaviour. If the two characters successfully hide their feelings and resist the urge to react in some way, there is no story. But if they let their feelings show, if their words and actions betray them and an interaction starts to take place, the story has begun.

And you have begun to outline the structure. Quite simply, this is the outline of the story, from beginning to end. A sequence of events, each dependent upon the last, each dependent also upon the characters involved. Because she's insecure, she will react in *this* particular way; because he feels guilty, he'll respond like *that*. And so it goes on: a chain reaction. Nothing must happen that is out of character, yet the story must take its different twists and turns to keep the line of suspense taut and the reader hooked.

Remember that the other essence of any story is conflict. When emotions run high, people say and do things that in calmer times they might not. Her indignation leads to his anger, aggravating her to fury, and so on. From an argument comes action, from action come consequences... A story is born.

Think through your plot in this way, always letting the characters act as befits their own psychology. It is infuriating, as a reader, to see a character behaving in a way that you know they just wouldn't have done. And readers do know. Just as they recognise body language, so they understand when a character's actions or words don't ring true.

It may be tempting sometimes to force your characters into a situation just because it strikes you as a 'good' one. But if it doesn't chime in with their personalities, it won't work, no matter how dramatic or touching the situation is. Leave it out; promise yourself you'll use it another time, in another book. If it's especially good, perhaps it should actually *be* your next book.

## Pacing your story

How can you be sure that you have enough for a full book? Reckon on a 60,000 word book having about ten to twelve chapters. That makes a chapter about 5,000–6,000 words long. Take a sheet of paper and jot down chapter headings – one to ten, or twelve. (You may end up with nine or eleven, but this doesn't matter.) If you prefer, use filing cards, a separate one for each chapter.

For each chapter, note the main events of the story as they occur. Each chapter in itself should have its own shape; it should deal with one major development of the story. It should follow on from the one before and lead on to the next, but there must be a moment of change within that chapter. At the same time, it should point the way to the next by ending in 'cliff-hanger' style, with another new or impending crisis.

Suppose you can't think of enough situations to stretch to a full book?

Dee Williams (author of *Hannah of Hope Street*, etc.) has a solution: 'Give your protagonist another problem. It can come in the form of another character, or strong feelings he or she has, or a very real situation, but it must fit in with your story and not detract from the plot. Remember, as with any problem, you must be able to solve it sensibly and realistically before the end.'

Bringing in another character adds another dimension to the story but, as Dee says, the new character must fit in – you can't let the story go off at a tangent. There should be a strong emotional link with one of the main characters, which will affect the situation between the two of them. And the direction of the story should be changed by this new character, adding to the complications and making it harder to resolve – and therefore stronger.

The same goes for a new situation – something coming out of the blue, like a sudden illness in the family, or financial problems. Anything that needs urgent attention must have an effect on the main storyline. It may create further conflict, or it may help to resolve feelings, but if it doesn't have a real effect, it mustn't be brought in. You can't just toss in another problem that is then tackled and solved without having had any effect on the outcome of the main plot.

As well as believing that there must be a secret formula, some beginners think that there has to be a defined 'shape' to any novel. To a certain extent, this is true. The shape of a novel isn't found by drawing a graph and making the story fit the peaks and troughs. Clearly, if you are going to structure your novel and not work 'by instinct' – as some writers claim to do – you will want to work out the high spots and the lows. Punctuate your story with little climaxes. Build up the tension with conflict, until a climax occurs. Look at the consequence of this climax and start again, building up further tension and so on, until you reach the grand climax at the end of the book. The important thing is to make sure that each subsequent problem, and each climax is greater than the one before. The progression must be on an upward line. The problems must get more difficult. This is what keeps the reader interested and makes the book 'unputdownable'. If you don't do this, you risk the story sagging, the reader becoming bored and the book being all too easy to put down, never to be picked up again.

## Keeping track of characters and events

Sometimes, a book has to be very tightly worked out. As an example, let me show you how I wrote the 'Street At War' quartet. Because the stories were told against a very real, well-documented and well-remembered background, the details had to be accurate. Most of the stories, following the lives of a group of people, depended on what was happening in the war – nationally, internationally and locally. The books were, in fact, a number of separate stories, not following the rule that all the plots must affect each other, but written more like a soap opera, a kind of *Coronation Street*. Nevertheless, they were all bound by the constraints of the war.

With a vague idea of who my characters were going to be, I started to research. I used a number of different sources and set down all my findings day by day, month by month, year by year, picking out anything that I thought would be useful, interesting or vital in the final writing. I did this on my computer, using a different font for each source, so that I could easily identify and go back to it if necessary. I looked again at my characters and saw how their stories could develop – this one joining the Land Army, that one taken prisoner of war, another killed by a flying bomb – and I added these pointers at the appropriate dates. This system made it very clear what was happening to any character at any time, so that I could also weave their stories together where possible. By the time I had finished, I had a very thorough outline of the story and was able to start writing.

I printed it all out and kept it beside me as a guideline. Without this, such a complex book could easily have degenerated into chaos, particularly when the characters began to 'live' and tell their own stories.

Another writer might use sheets of coloured paper to differentiate between research sources or characters. Another might pin pages of description or 'character fact-sheets' on the wall. I once tried huge spreadsheets, with dates and cross-checking, but it was so big it took up all of one wall and so complicated I never referred to it. We all develop the ways in which we work best.

Generally, I would say that the hard work you put into the preparation will pay off in the writing. It is enormously frustrating to have to keep flicking through a pile of papers and cuttings, or search through a collection of books. It made it so much simpler for me to have my guidelines beside me, allowing me to get on and write.

## Is there a formula?

For pure romance, there is a fairly well recognised and accepted structure – and this is what people call a *formula*. It is easy to discover what this is simply by reading a number of such books, but don't mistake detail and storyline for structure and get bogged down with how many pages there are before the first kiss and so on. It isn't that stereotyped. Just decide whether your story fits in with this genre and then write it. If it doesn't fit, either give it some more thought, or write it the way you believe it should be written. Don't try to force a story into a genre to which it doesn't belong.

The romantic novel, with its broader scope, has fewer rules. It may take one of several forms; a contemporary story, a family saga, a historical epic – anything, in fact, that is written with an essential core of emotion. The emotional experiences and development of the characters are paramount.

## Summary

- Make a chapter-by-chapter outline.
- Make sure sub-plots are crucial to the main storyline.
- Keep your characters and what happens to them clear in your mind.

# 7

# THE MIDDLE AND THE END

## Fleshing it out

Sometimes an editor will complain that a story needs 'fleshing out' or 'beefing up'. (Editors talk in these oddly carnivorous terms.) This means that you've stuck too closely to the bones (there we go again) and probably that the narrative is too stark, without enough colour or warmth. Perhaps there's not enough dialogue; almost certainly there isn't enough action, and what there is seems pale and uninteresting.

Sketching out each chapter before you begin to write will show you if you have enough story. If this is your first effort at writing a book, you may find it difficult to assess just how much room you will need to develop each different stage of the plot. This is something that comes with experience, but you should be able to tell if your chapters are going to be on the thin side, or if they are plump and juicy and bursting with story.

If any of your chapters do look thin, or you've run out of story by chapter eight, you will need to rethink your plot. Perhaps it is too straightforward and you need to introduce some complications. Another character, as Dee Williams suggests, might be enough – but that character must have an effect on the main storyline. And this means an effect on your heroine, since she is the main character.

The new character will not necessarily drop neatly into place in the middle of chapter eight, just where you've begun to run out of plot. If you do that, the 'join' will be horribly visible and the story won't flow. You may need to look further back into the story and set up your new character much earlier. You might even have to bring in a sub-plot to support him or her, and you may need more than one new character –

so the complications are already beginning, and you can see that the story is already gaining new momentum.

The new situation must be woven in with the main plot, so tightly that the reader cannot imagine one happening without the other. It's not like a TV soap; there, the stories happen in parallel, as neighbours living in the same street or village live out their separate stories. In a saga, this may be perfectly all right and I shall discuss this later, but in the short romance it can't be allowed to happen. The romance, being a story of cause and effect, is more like what happens when someone sells a house and buys another. Unless you are very lucky, you find yourself involved in a complicated chain that might extend halfway round the country – and what Family A do, up in Edinburgh, filters right down through the chain and affects you, nine houses onwards, in south Devon. Worse still, one spanner thrown in the works by Family B or E can wreck the whole complex process.

This is why it is so useful to map out your book chapter by chapter. If you've begun to write and got all the way to chapter eight before thinking about this, you will not only have expended a lot of energy and time, but you will also have become very involved with your characters. They will have developed as people. The story will have developed too and may have changed along the way, and all this will make it more difficult to go back and introduce new material.

It can be done, of course. But I am all for making the task of writing as easy as possible (while not ducking the difficulties!) and if you can start writing with a good, strong storyline, mapped out chapter by chapter, beside you, the other problems you encounter will be that much less.

Your new character can't be a puppet, any more than your main characters are. He is a new person, with his own agenda, and what he does will – *must* – affect the main storyline and send it shooting off in a different direction. But he must not, in a romance, distract from the main purpose, which is the love story between the hero and heroine. He must be closely concerned with it.

This is why the extra character in a romance is often 'another man' or 'another woman'. Such a character has an emotional effect – and romances are all about emotion. Or you might have a mother or other relative who exerts a powerful influence on either the hero or the heroine.

This brings me back to Kate and her little girl. Very early on in my writing days I was advised that, if you include a child in a story, she must play an important part. She's not there just for 'cuteness'. And children aren't easy to write – Joanna Trollope (author of *The Rector's Wife*, *Next of Kin*, etc.) is one who writes children marvellously, and her children add a dimension of enormous tenderness to her books. But it is not easy to achieve such delightful 'childlikeness'. More often, a child will come over as being irritatingly precocious or sickeningly sentimental.

I tried to avoid this in my Mills & Boon romance *Unfinished Business*. The child was the hero's small daughter, Lucy. I felt that to make her interesting she must have her own definite character, and her own interests, and hit upon the idea of letting her be obsessed with rabbits. She had her own family, headed by Mr and Mrs MacGregor, and her life revolved around these rabbits. When asked by the heroine, Verity, if she were breeding them, she answered in all seriousness, 'No, they're doing it themselves' – and this remark set the tone for all the scenes involving Lucy throughout the book. And it gave me a chance to show the hero in a softer light as he resignedly helped to build pens and racecourses for the rabbit gymkhana.

If Kate in our example storyline is to have a child to support, the child must feature strongly in the story, and have her own characteristics, her own storyline. Lucy's rabbits ran neatly alongside the main story but she was unknowingly deeply involved in the conflict and resolution between the hero and heroine. Polly too has her own life, her own concerns, but she should have a vital part to play in the story itself. That doesn't mean it has to be a big part, but it must be crucial. A story involving a child is a three-way story.

## It's getting too long!

In a way, this is a good fault – at least you haven't got to struggle to think of new situations. But you will have to exert some discipline on a story that threatens to overflow its pages. You may find that your writing is too exuberant and needs to be curbed. Or you may realise that there is just too much plot and you need to cut down on some of the scenes; some might be able to be shown 'off-stage', some might have to be cut altogether. Clearly, you will only do this with scenes that are not essential to the plot, are not between the hero and heroine or are not particularly good scenes anyway.

Remember, however, that, as you work through the story and possibly change your mind or develop new ideas, older scenes can become less relevant. Keep looking back to see if this is the case, and be prepared to rewrite.

Cutting can be done in a number of ways. First, try to look at your story with a coldly objective eye and decide whether it works as it is. It might help to write a synopsis or precis. Do all the scenes lead one from another, flowing so naturally and so tightly that you really couldn't cut any of them without detracting from the story? Are there any parts left over from previous thinking that don't seem so relevant now? Have you repeated a theme or development? Do you have any scenes that are similar to each other?

Anything that can be cut in this way, should be cut – even if the story isn't too long. Irrelevancies are irritating, and will lose you your readers. But suppose you've done all that and it's still too long – what then?

Look once more at the storyline. There may be a sub-plot that you can do without. Even if you've followed the rules so far, and the sub-plot is integral to the main plot, it may still be possible to cut it down, or even drop it altogether. There may be another, shorter way of making the story work. This may mean some serious rewriting, because if you've done your job properly the sub-plot will be tightly woven in and difficult to extricate. You'll have to be very careful to weed out all the references and allusions. It will probably mean dropping one or more characters as well. Not something to be undertaken lightly, but some-times it is the only way.

If the storyline is really tight and cutting of this sort would damage it, you must look at your writing – indeed, you should be looking at your writing all the time. But it is surprising how easy it is to overwrite without realising it.

When *The Girls They Left Behind* was edited, I was appalled (and so, I imagine, was my editor) to discover just how many rhetorical questions I had allowed my characters to ask. (That's the great thing about letting your characters take over – you can blame them when things go wrong.) These were all questions that were asked inside people's heads, through their thoughts. It's a common device in romances, where the story is seen so much through one person's eyes, but it was out of place in the wartime saga.

I went right through the manuscript, weeding out all these rhetorical questions and when I had finished I found that I had cut no less than *four thousand words*! And not one of them added anything useful to the story. Once cut, they left no mark because they just didn't matter.

You can do a lot of cutting, rephrasing, reorganising sentences, using plain English rather than convoluted phrases and long words, without losing any of the actual sense, without losing any of the action or any of the emotion. And your writing will be all the clearer for it, and all the more enjoyable to read.

If after all this your romance is still too long, and there really isn't anything you can do to cut it down any further, there is one more option you may consider. And that is whether it is a romance at all. Perhaps, all this time, you've really been writing a romantic novel.

## So – let's write a romantic novel

Much of what has been said about the romance applies equally to the romantic novel, or indeed any other kind of novel. You can't talk about one genre without giving general advice that applies to all.

The romantic novel is simply further down the road from the romance. I first began to see the difference when I had written a number of Mills & Boon romances and, while I enjoyed writing them and wanted to continue, I began to find there were subjects that just wouldn't do for this kind of light reading. I wanted something tougher – something seamier – to get my teeth into. Instead of – or I should say, *as well as* – optimistic fantasy that nevertheless stuck to its own truthful lines, I wanted to tell a different sort of truth. I wanted to present life as it is, or has been, rather than as we'd like it to be.

Some romances have tried to do this by including references to contraception and safe sex. 'On our way home, I just need to stop at the chemists,' the hero observes, making it clear what he has in mind and  making it equally clear that he doesn't go about prepared all the time, so he's not promiscuous. Or the heroine happens to be already on the pill, for 'medical reasons' (like not wanting to get pregnant?). But to me, these devices detract from the style of the romance. It takes away the spontaneity, the overwhelming sweep of passion that I believe is one of the ingredients the reader looks for. It introduces a sense of coldness.

I know that the idea is to instil responsibility. But the tradition of marriage did that, and the driving force of the romance has always been towards the total commitment of marriage. So, although the white wedding as a symbol of virginity has more or less gone by the board now, people still like the ceremony, the trappings, the symbolism of it all, the *commitment*. That's proven by the number of couples who have their register-office wedding blessed in church, and wear the same special clothes, have the same flower-decked brides-maids and the same reception as any traditional wedding.

I believe that this is what the reader of romances wants too: the sense that the couple whose fortunes they have been following are now totally committed to each other, to the extent of making wedding vows and having children.

But the romantic novel can look at the wider issues of life. The heroine need not marry the hero – or at least, not immediately. She may have other relationships, disastrous and mistaken ones, and so may he. You can talk openly about whatever sexually transmitted disease was the current scourge at the time of which you are writing. You can include other diseases and disasters. You can put your heroine through tragedies that would be just too strong for a romance. You can have several other strong characters with their own stories or sub-plots that will drive the story along.

This means that your construction will be much more intricate, but you can still work on the same lines, sketching out the main storyline to begin with and then breaking it down into chapters. You need to make decisions as you go along as to which characters will be the most important, what minor characters you need, and what the sub-plots will be. You may need to introduce one in order to help the main plot over a difficult patch, and new characters may come along with the new plot. Although it is quite possible to write a book without looking at all this beforehand, and tackling each issue as it arises – and there will inevitably be a certain amount of this happening anyway – it really is much easier to think through as much as you can before you begin the real writing. Any obstacles you face then will be minor in comparison to the huge ones you will encounter if you just leap in without any idea as to where you're heading.

You can also see that the shape is forming properly and that the sub-plots aren't becoming too prominent. Keep your main storyline to the forefront; it should occupy the greater part of each chapter. And keep your sub-plots in balance; they don't all have to be part of every chapter, but they do need to weave in and out as supporting strands of the whole pattern. They should touch each other in places, too, so that the entire fabric is interdependent.

The romantic novel is generally about 120,000–160,000 words, or possibly even longer. We keep hearing that doorstop novels are no longer wanted, but we keep seeing them on the bookshelves just the same. There is no real rule – a story is as long as it needs to be. You can follow the lines I have already suggested to keep it down, but in the end there is no more left to cut, no sub-plot to jettison, no word that is unnecessary. And if it's a good book, the publisher will want to publish it. But you do have to remember that there are publication costs – the amount of paper needed, the cost of printing, and so forth – so length does matter. Don't pad it out just to make it look good. (It won't.)

Length such as this is daunting enough anyway, and not only to the new writer. J. B. Priestley said that when he was writing *The Good Companions*, 'it was like lifting an elephant on to the desk every morning.' That's just what it feels like, but forget the grand total ahead of you, set yourself a realistic number of words to write each day, and gradually the white elephant on the left-hand side of your desk becomes a grey elephant on the right. The pile of blank paper grows less and the typed paper more. And – if you've done your homework thoroughly beforehand – surprisingly quickly.

The greater span of the romantic novel gives you room to go more deeply into your characters' lives. Because you can use several different viewpoint characters, you can show the interplay between them, and give the reader an insight that the pure romance may not be able to achieve. I have always admired the American writer Helen Van Slyke, who can show the thoughts and feelings of one character so convincingly that the reader can't help but sympathise – and then go on and do exactly the same with an opposing character, so that we are equally caught up with them. What she is showing us is that we are all human beings, with faults and frailties and a valid point of view, seen from our own perspective. Not a bad thing to remember in our own everyday lives!

You may decide to follow this example and devote a chapter at a time, or even an entire section, to one viewpoint. That can be very interesting. It gets your reader deeply involved with each character and enables you to take a global view. Its disadvantage is that when you have to make the break, the reader is likely to experience a moment of disruption – she's grown interested in Little Red Riding Hood and what she's getting up to with the woodcutter, and doesn't really want to go off with the wolf to granny's house. But if you're doing your job properly, the disruption will be only momentary. The wolf too is an interesting character and so is granny, and the reader knows that what happens between them is going to affect LRRH as well, so she stays with it.

Your other choice is to deal with a number of viewpoint characters in each chapter, in soap-opera style. You don't have to include every character or every sub-plot, but you do need to be weaving in two or three as well as the main story, and you must keep them in balance and let them overlap, so that the reader is led gently from one to another without realising it. Sudden resolutions of one story and abrupt beginnings to the next will bring about that disruption again, less validly this time, and it isn't how life works.

Sub-plots don't occur in neat little bundles. They run unevenly. One may simmer quietly in the background for a while before erupting again, another may tear like a raging hurricane through two or three chapters and then blow itself out. But you must still keep that balance between them; don't let the plot on the back-burner disappear altogether while the hurricane is raging.

However carefully you work out your storyline beforehand, you are still likely to find that some plots don't work when you come to put them into writing, or that others that you hadn't even thought of start to surface. If this happens, don't push them away, thinking you have to stick to your plan. It can always be reworked. But neither should you just blunder on, hoping it will all work out right in the end.

P. G. Wodehouse, writing to his friend Bill Townsend (*Performing Flea*), observed once that he had 'now reached a point where deep thought is required'. Wodehouse's stories are as tightly plotted as any you are likely to come across, yet he shows over and over again that in his writing he still remained fluid and open to change.

# Endings

Once you have written your romance or romantic novel, you have to end it. The reader of a romance wants to see the couple wander off hand-in-hand into the sunset. But if she is reading the wider-ranging romantic novel, she won't necessarily expect a happy ending.

Jessica Stirling (author of *Gates of Midnight*, *Hearts of Gold*, etc.) says: 'Isn't it odd that the most famous and enduring romantic novels do *not* end Happily Ever After but are sealed either by death or irrevocable parting.

'Poignancy, I suppose, is the crucial element that parting adds to romance, together with a sense of completeness that the demise of one of the lovers, or of the affair itself, brings to a novel. The love affair thereafter is encased in memory and protected against the inevitable diminishing of passion that even the most starry-eyed reader knows is bound to occur if a storyline is extended too far.

'Almost all classic and enduring love stories are closed off in this manner, from *Wuthering Heights* through *Anna Karenina* and Hemingway's *A Farewell To Arms* into more contrived best-sellers like *Love Story*, *The Bridges of Madison County* and *The Horse Whisperer*.'

However, Jessica warns against artificial manipulation: 'Just knocking off the hero or heroine on page 242 is not enough to guarantee that posterity, or Hollywood, will come knocking at your door. The *reasons* for ending the relationship must not detract *in any way* from a reader's sympathy for either of the lovers. One or both characters may be flawed but neither should be depicted as culpable when it comes to a parting. Motivation must seem entirely credible while a 'no-choice' situation, like the soft, slow tightening of a knot, is being skilfully drawn into the plot.'

Jessica warns that all this is 'easy to say, not so easy to do. It takes nerve to deliberately aim a novel at a poignant ending. But for my money it's certainly where the biggest and best love stories come from.'

Notice too how Jessica Stirling defines a romantic novel. It is a sadness to me, and to many others, that the perception of this term seems to have become focused on what I am calling pure romance. For millions of satisfied readers, there is nothing at all wrong with romance. But the romantic novel takes in a far wider range, represented by some of the finest classical authors and probably enjoyed by many of the same readers. It's a shame that the two are confused, to the detriment of both. And a shame that readers of romance are sometimes deemed to be unable to read anything else!

Sheila Walsh agrees: 'A romantic novel can be a traditional love story, movingly told. But it can also be much more. At its most ambitious, it may encompass a whole range of human emotions – greed, jealousy, ambition, retribution, even tragedy. But throughout, love must be at the core of the story, making it, until the last triumphant page, unputdownable.'

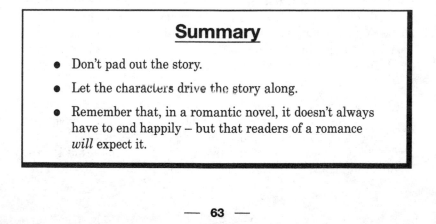

# Summary

- Don't pad out the story.

- Let the characters drive the story along.

- Remember that, in a romantic novel, it doesn't always have to end happily – but that readers of a romance *will* expect it.

# 8

# BRINGING THE STORY TO LIFE

## <u>Suspense</u>

Suspense is created by never giving quite all the answers. That doesn't mean you can cheat – anything your hero or heroine knows should be available to the reader. But as he or she is searching for resolutions to the situation, so the reader too must wonder what is going to happen. Again, build up each crisis so that instead of getting better, it gets more difficult. Then the reader will be unable to put down the book until she knows all is well.

Suspense also depends on the reader's interest in the characters. A lively human being, who engages our interest and enthusiasm, will begin to matter to us. We want to know what happens to him or her. We want to keep reading.

Suspense can also be created by using flashback. You can hold back a certain piece of information by leap-frogging events and then returning to tell that part of the story from an earlier point. This will create a certain pleasurable frustration in the reader, who just *has* to read on. If the reader knows already what is going to happen, the suspense can be almost greater than if they don't know. It is especially useful if you feel the story might sag at this point: you can condense awkward spans of time and lift the action. But don't do it too often, or it will become irritating.

You can do this for any length from a couple of pages to the entire book. It has been done to great effect by Ruth Rendell in *A Judgement in Stone*, where we know that an appalling event is inevitable yet still find ourselves begging for it not to happen. Nevil Shute did it in a slightly different way, in *Requiem for a Wren*, where we know from the outset that the girl has killed herself, and are then taken through the events which led up to her suicide.

These are examples in which a story is made more effective through not being told chronologically. The structure of the book is not really very different, since the flashback takes up almost the entire book. You just have to remember that you are working towards an end that you have already read, at the beginning. Obviously, such books must be carefully plotted.

Flashback is also useful when you arrive at a climax but don't want to go into all the details of the subsequent events immediately afterwards, if these are rather laborious and uninteresting. In this case, you can leap ahead to the next point at which the story begins to move again, and just let your characters discuss the previous events briefly, thus getting over any information that the reader ought to have. Or you can have one character recalling them in thought. In other words, it's a good way of condensing time.

Chapter endings can be a great help in building suspense. Each should be a mini-climax – but not a resolution. Each should be seen to lead immediately to further complications, so that the reader – who has perhaps decided to read to the end of the chapter before doing the washing-up – doesn't put the book down, but turns the page and goes on reading. If you are really working well, she won't move until she's finished the entire book. This is of course rare. I can remember only two books that actually kept me rooted to my chair until I had finished: William Golding's *Lord of the Flies*, and a wonderful children's book by Ann Holm called *I Am David*. But there have been plenty I've put down very reluctantly and found my thoughts straying to constantly until I could pick them up again.

The enjoyment of a story doesn't stop just because the book has been laid aside. A good story will go with the reader, possibly for the rest of her life. A memorable character seems almost to become part of the reader, as it was a part of the writer. Perhaps this is what we subconsciously look for when we pick up a book to read – something that will reach out from the page and become a part of us. Perhaps, as writers, we are struggling to communicate something from deep within, to touch people we shall never meet.

If this sounds pretentious I make no apology. There are as many different readers as there are books, and we all have different needs and different ways of satisfying them. A slim paperback romance might touch one person as deeply as a heavy tome of literature might touch another. It is for no one to judge the needs and satisfactions of someone else.

I have never forgotten hearing a radio interview – better expressed as a confrontation, perhaps – on *Woman's Hour*, between Irma Kurtz and Jacqui Bianchi, a senior editor at Mills & Boon. Jacqui was my own editor at that time so I knew that she was a tiny person with a very soft voice. Irma Kurtz, who clearly had little time for Mills & Boon, asked rather scornfully if, in this day and age, liberated women oughtn't to be discouraged from reading such trashy books. To which Jacqui, softly and sweetly, answered: 'I would have thought that liberation meant that a woman should be able to read exactly what she damned well likes.'

Brilliant.

# Viewpoint

Almost all writers must be aware that there are a number of viewpoints from which the story can be told. In practice there are two. There is the first-person it-happened-to-me viewpoint and the third-person viewpoint which still sees the story through the eyes of one character (or one at a time).

Every story is, in a way, about every character involved in it. They each have their own point of view, their own feelings, and each will be affected in some way – perhaps for the rest of their (fictional) lives. But the writer has to make choices. Someone has to be the main character – and this is obviously the person to whom the main thread of the story is happening. In a romance, there are clearly going to be two main characters, in the wider-ranging romantic novel probably more, although one will carry the main burden of the story. These are the characters whose viewpoints we want to see.

In the pure romance, there isn't space to probe deeply into the minds of more than one character, neither is it desirable. And ninety-five per cent of the time, this main character will be the heroine. Hers are the thoughts and feelings the reader is interested in. She it is with whom the reader wants to identify completely and there is usually no need to see into anyone else's mind.

As a rule, these stories are told in the third person. It seems better for the reader to be able to see the heroine as a separate person, even while wanting close identification. Physical description, too, is easier to give through a third-person viewpoint. It is difficult to have a heroine say things like: 'My green eyes gleamed'. The third-person viewpoint gives the freedom of seeing things through the heroine's eyes, while at the same time being able to step slightly aside when necessary.

The first person does have its uses, however. You can give the reader an even deeper sense of identification and you avoid having to keep pointing out that the heroine is 'thinking'. A lot of action stories are told in the first person. But it does restrict you. The reader can only know what the main character knows.

Occasionally, you will find a romance that devotes a chapter or so to the hero's viewpoint, and even less frequently you will find one told entirely from the hero's point of view – sometimes with great success. But it isn't common, and it's probably best to start conventionally rather than breaking the rules with your first book. (This patronising statement is, of course, certain to provoke the wilder spirits amongst you to break every rule you can find.)

The romantic novel will often take several characters as viewpoint characters. These will always be the ones most deeply involved in or directly affecting the lives (and stories) of the main characters, and the amount of the story told through their eyes will be in proportion to their importance. The difficulty here comes when you have two of these characters together. Whose viewpoint do you use then?

I have my own loose rules about this. There is, amongst these characters, a sort of pecking order. The main character comes at the top, the next most important – probably the potential lover – just below, and so on. In any scene where these characters are interacting together, the main character would usually take precedence. The same goes all the way down the hierarchy.

An exception is where the scene actually *belongs* to the minor character. In this scene, it is the lesser character who is the moving force in the story at that point, or who is changing in a way that is important to the story. It would be wrong at this point not to give this character the importance that the story itself dictates.

Where two minor viewpoint characters are together, look at whose part of the story this scene is concerned with. That person is the viewpoint character. It's probably best not to switch viewpoints back and forth during their exchanges. But you can start a scene with one character and end it with the second, particularly if you have them parting. In such a situation, you simply go off with the second character and hear his thoughts on the subject. But only if it is useful for the story. It is perfectly permissible to have someone who is one of the viewpoint characters not showing his thoughts. (For one thing, he may not have any useful ones, just at that point.) These are moments at which you have to make your own choices.

## Tenses

Most stories are told in the past tense, as a series of events that have already taken place. This is simple enough and you can see examples in almost every book you open. It's the most common way of telling a story.

Sometimes, it is necessary to slip into the pluperfect sense. This is when you have to insert the word 'had' into every verb, which can be very irritating. Normally, you need to use the pluperfect because you have gone into a flashback. For example: 'Mary stood at the window, her heart beating quickly. She remembered the last time she had seen John. They had gone down to the beach together...'

Now, this may be quite brief and there's no problem, but you may have quite a long episode to recount that takes place entirely in Mary's thoughts. You may even include dialogue as well as action, and as we have already seen, a flashback can sometimes take up the entire book. You can see how tedious it will be if you have to insert 'had' into every sentence, perhaps more than once.

The good news is that it isn't necessary. Flashback can be handled perfectly well without doing this. All you need is to use the pluperfect for the first two or three sentences and then drop it until you come back out of the flashback to 'close' the episode neatly. The reader won't notice, and wouldn't blame you if she did. She doesn't want to read all those 'hads' any more than you want to write them.

What about present-tense stories? I have to say that I am not very keen on stories told in the present tense and have been known to put them down as soon as I realise! I can never quite stop myself from wondering how this narrator is managing to tell the story while running for his life – in other words, I can't suspend my disbelief.

However my prejudice doesn't mean that the present tense isn't a perfectly valid way of telling a story. Two excellent recent books have been written in this way – *Miss Smilla's Feeling for Snow*, by Peter Hoeg, and *Deceit*, by Clare Francis.

A friend who is also a writer and has read both these books, tells me she liked them so much she has started her new book in the same style. But I still feel that, for me at any rate, there has to be a good reason to tell a particular story in this way – a reason so good that to tell it conventionally just would not work.

The use of the present tense prevents the narrator from knowing what happens next, as a past-tense narrator clearly must know. And it may also deceive the reader as to the nature of the narrator himself. For instance, I can recall two stories – a chilling short story by Charlotte Perkins Gilman called *The Yellow Wallpaper*, and a novel by Thomas Hinde called *The Day The Call Came*, neither of which could have been told in any other way.

## Ways of telling the story

Most novels are told chronologically and in the past tense, with events told as they might be by one person to another, in real life. But there are other ways of telling a story too. Some are written as diaries, with the story unfolding through the entries. This prevents the 'now I'm sitting down to tell the story of what happened' syndrome. In *The Brimstone Wedding*, Ruth Rendell uses a very interesting form in which the story is told as it happens, yet in the past tense. It's not a diary, but neither is it told entirely as in the past, with all the

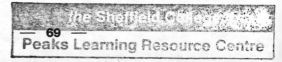

hindsight that such a telling must have. It's more as if the narrator is recounting the events to a friend as they happen, day by day.

Keeping the tenses right in this sort of telling is tricky, but Ruth Rendell is a mistress of unusual writing and never fails to make it work.

Sometimes the story can be told through letters, though this is not much favoured these days and it isn't really suitable for the romance genre. But that isn't to say that such a book would never be accepted. It depends very much on your own skill, and on your reasons.

Sometimes you have to work out a structure that is specific to a particular book. I had to do this for my historical novel *Bid Time Return*, with its theme of patterns recurring through three generations of the same family. This meant I had three main characters to begin with, one for each part of the story. The third and last (Joanna) was to experience, through a kind of time-shift device, the lives of her two predecessors.

I had to think a bit about this. I didn't want the story to be told chronologically, because I didn't think this would work. In the end, I started the book with Joanna and told the early part of her story before slipping into the first time-shift. We then saw Louisa's life. Then it was back to Joanna, picking up from where we had left her – but after having had this strange dreamlike experience – and went on with her story before slipping back again into the experiences of Rupert. Finally, we returned to Joanna for the remainder of her story and the denouement that brought her neatly back to Louisa, though in a different way.

But I didn't write it just like that. I wrote only a short part of Joanna's early story first, to set the tone of the book. Then I wrote Louisa's story, and then Rupert's. Only then, with all the knowledge of what had happened in the 'past', was I able to complete all the parts of Joanna's story. I could not have done it before, because so much was still hidden from me.

## Show and tell

Show and tell are the two main ways of conveying a story to your reader. They each have their place, and you are likely to employ both during the course of your book. But you will probably find that you tend to favour one rather than the other.

This may be something you need to look at and possibly change. Too much telling, and the story is compressed and tends to read like a police report. Too much showing, and you'll never get to the end.

Telling is when you simply write factually about what happened. 'Mary stood at the window, her heart beating quickly.' Well, presumably emotion is there, unless Mary had been running or jumping on the spot, or doing something equally strenuous. But it is only implicit. Perhaps Mary *had* just finished an exercise routine. We need a bit more information to be able to complete our picture.

'Mary stood at the window, her heart beating quickly, her thoughts in turmoil.' Ah. Running on the spot isn't likely to have had that effect. But so far the writer is still only *telling* the reader how Mary feels. 'Mary stood at the window and raised one hand to her mouth, nibbling on fingernails she had already bitten almost to the quick.' We haven't said anything about the state of her thoughts, but the reader knows she's nervous – and not just at this moment. She's a habitually nervous person. Nail-biting is a habit, which people either do or don't do.

You see how much work this sentence does for you? Not only do we know what Mary is doing at this moment, we know how she's feeling and we know a little bit more about Mary as a person. And we know this in the best way possible – from our own understanding of how people behave. We've been shown, and we're able to take it from there.

It is far more enjoyable for a reader to be able to do some of the work herself, to bring her own insights and understanding to what you have written. You don't need to cross every t and dot every i. Showing often avoids this risk.

This is not to say that you must always paint a word picture. Long, wordy descriptions of the way people look and their surroundings are not showing – that's just telling, dressed up. Showing is displaying behaviour or action so that the reader understands without being told. We haven't said that Mary is a nervy person, but her action while standing at the window – which is a development in the story itself –

clearly shows this, and the reader will not forget. But if you simply said 'Mary was a nervous person' not only would it probably seem stilted and intrusive, it would not be memorable. It would not fix this characteristic of Mary's in the reader's mind.

Don't think, however, that there is no place for telling. Sometimes, showing can slow the action. Saying that Mary is a nervous person takes up fewer words and therefore less time than describing her bitten nails. When you are building suspense, it's often a good idea to do it slowly, so that the reader is almost crying with frustration – in the best possible sense. Showing at these times increases the tension and gets the reader even more deeply into the characters' minds. But later, when you are building to a climax, you may find that telling works better. Straight reporting, of either actions or emotional responses, can impart the sense of urgency you need.

In the example I have quoted earlier, of the lunch party in *Rebecca*, Daphne du Maurier employs straight telling techniques. The dialogue is almost Hemingwayesque in its crisp baldness, and no mention is made of the emotions of those taking part. Yet, as in Hemingway, you know that beneath the surface emotions of the deepest, most desperate nature are surging like lava in a volcano about to erupt. You know exactly what each person must be feeling. To be shown such deep emotions graphically would take the scene right over the top and would diminish the tension.

Most writers fall into one of the two categories – they are either show writers or tell writers. They favour one method or the other and find that one easier to do. It doesn't really matter which you are, because it's all a part of having your own voice, but you need to know which you are best at, and to improve your skills in the other, in order to tell your story in the best possible way.

Tell writers will nearly always write 'too short'. They find it difficult to manage a long novel or even a short story, and may be told to 'put some flesh on the bones'. They're brilliant at mini-sagas but can't understand how to expand a storyline. They're often better at non-fiction, and may give up on the idea of writing a novel.

This may be the case. Some of us *are* better at non-fiction. But the fact that you are reading this book surely means that you must have stories teeming in your head, ideas for plots, characters who want to be out there on the page. You want to be a fiction writer.

So, what to do if you recognise yourself as a tell writer?

Read through a piece of your writing. A thousand words or so should be enough to start with. Look at all the times you have described a piece of action, however small. Have you said simply, 'He walked across the room'? There may be nothing wrong with that at all. It may be exactly right for that moment. But see if it makes any difference to use a different word than 'walk' – strut, stalk, amble, march, hobble. Already we have been given a picture.

Is there anything else you can do to add to this picture? He could toss his head, flick back his hair, shake his fist, take a pen out of his top pocket, clutch his heart, blow his nose – whatever is right for the moment you're describing. And what about his expression – is he glowering, smiling, snarling or lifting one eyebrow in that oddly seductive way some film stars can?

I think you're getting the idea now. Go through the rest of your piece, doing the same thing. And don't just apply it to the action. As we've seen before, people rarely sit quite still. If they do, it's worth a mention in itself. But usually they fidget about, shifting this way and that, leaning their elbows on the table, resting their chins in their hands, staring at other people staring away from other people, rubbing their eyes, pushing back their hair, clasping their hands together – and as often as not, these movements betray some hidden emotion or reaction to the person they're with or the situation they're in.

Use these movements. Use the environment. And remember that the reader doesn't know everything that you know – it's easy to forget to make it clear. I've sometimes written a scene in which, on rereading it, I discover that there is no mention at all as to where the characters are. They could be on the moon for all the reader knows. I've been so wrapped up in the action that I've forgotten to put them on stage – or to give them scenery when they're there. I know where they are but I've forgotten that the reader doesn't.

Every morning, when you wake up, you look around your room and see things. Every day, when you step out of your house, you notice your environment. You are aware of where you are. You feel the breeze, you know what the temperature is, you smell exhaust fumes, or manure, or seaweed, or roses. You hear traffic, or seagulls, or cows. You see whatever produces these sounds and these smells. You can fix yourself in your piece of the world.

So must the reader be able to fix your characters in their place. So tell the reader what to see, hear and smell. Better still, show her. Bring that scene vividly to life, and your characters will live as well, because a cardboard puppet will not work against real scenery. You will have to make your people real too; you won't be able to help yourself.

Show writing puts the flesh on the bones, without padding.

## Emotional warmth

Above all, a romantic novel must contain that essential warmth and genuine emotion that can only be conveyed by knowing, understanding and liking your characters.

And here is the basic recipe for success – an interest in, liking for and understanding of real people, and a desire to convey those insights and emotions to readers through characters you have created. Or, as one novelist put it to me: sheer nosiness!

I think she was being hard on herself. But listen to what Pamela Oldfield (author of *The Butterfly Box*, *Lady of the Night*, etc.) has to say: 'Readers of a romantic novel want to be *emotionally* involved; they want to experience the romance. The writer must persuade them to care so deeply for the two main characters (male and female) that they suffer with them. They need, firstly, to feel the attraction the characters have for each other, to *know* that they are right for each other and to be longing for the moment when they finally get together – the happy ending. Always consider what you are writing from the reader's point of view and ask yourself if you are involving them fully. Let your readers feel the bitterness of rejection, the anguish of lost love, the guilt of betrayal as well as the excited anticipation of a clandestine meeting, the wonderful moment of sudden hope and the final joy of requited love...'

This is what is meant by emotional warmth. There are elements in such a story that many readers will recognise. And if your characters are drawn well enough, the reader will empathise with them – even when they are acting mistakenly. To achieve this, you need to be able to get right into your characters' skins yourself, so that you can convey your own understanding, and you will find that they behave like real people in a very human situation.

What about the girl with the disastrous wedding day?

I wrote this as a Mills & Boon novel called *Last Goodbye*. The heroine glimpses her new husband kissing the photograph of a beautiful girl. The honeymoon is spoiled as he insists that it was a last goodbye to his previous fiancée, who is now dead. But he refuses to discuss her death, and when the heroine sees her in the Devonshire town where they live, she can only assume that he is lying.

Imagine how she feels, how she will react; how he, knowing the truth but unable to reveal it, will react to her reactions.

The conflict need not always be between people. In *Moonlight and Love Songs*, the major conflict is an inner one, experienced by a girl who is deeply in love with her husband but, because of the extraordinary pressures on her, finds this love harshly tested. From living a normal, everyday life, she has been flung into situations she had never dreamed of and the story relates how she grapples to come to terms with these upheavals.

Again, the keynote is warmth – the human side of great events and what they could mean in our own lives.

*Moonlight and Love Songs*, despite its title, is not simply a 'romance'. But there is a strong thread of emotion running through it, and it is largely this thread, and the suspense involved in it, that holds the book together. And this applies to many stories that do not even claim to be romantic novels. There is often a thread of emotion on which the plot hangs, and it is as much the resolution of romantic conflict that determines the structure of the story as it is any other theme, such as crime, suspense or jeopardy etc.

# Summary

- Suspense comes from not giving all the answers at once.

- Use page breaks and chapter endings to add suspense.

- Change viewpoints only when there is good reason.

- Show writing adds impact, tell writing gives information.

- The mainspring of a romance or romantic novel is emotion.

# 9
# ROMANCE AND SEX

## So what is romance?

We've been bandying the term 'romance' around quite a lot. But what exactly is it? Is there one specific definition, or is it – as I suspect it may be – many things to many people?

I have differentiated between the pure romance as a story and the romantic novel. But that doesn't mean they don't have many things in common, and most important of these is romance.

In its broadest sense, romance is much more than glances meeting across a crowded room, hands touching accidentally across the table, and the tentative first overtures that will lead to love. It's more than the steamy love scene, the torrid affair, the stormy misunderstandings.

Iris Gower (author of *The Wild Seed*, *Firebird*, etc.) agrees that the term 'romance' encompasses a wide spectrum but adds that the reader always expects to find a good story, well told. 'Fine narrative writing is wonderful,' she says, 'but without strong characters, believable dialogue and imaginative plot development, fine writing falls flat on its face.'

'A good story' can also mean adventure. High adventure, such as is told in the stories of Walter Scott, Robert Louis Stevenson, H. Rider Haggard. *Ivanhoe* is a romance. So are *Kidnapped* and *King Solomon's Mines*. And although these books may be written in a style that seems old-fashioned now, the stories themselves remain swashbuckling adventures that translate readily to other media such as cinema and TV. And there will, almost invariably, be a man-woman element, a love affair that is the heart of the story. This element is the heart of life itself, the stuff that makes the world go round. *Of course* it's going to be included.

A romantic novel is any story that tells of important events in the life of a character or series of characters, through a logical sequence of incidents, raising a question at the beginning that will be answered by the end of the book. It is the story of a quest. There will always be an element of sexual love. In the romance, this must end at a happy moment (not necessarily happy ever after), but in the broader scope of the romantic novel, this does not have to be the case. The tragic conclusion may be a truer end, and will reverberate far longer in the reader's mind.

Someone once remarked that romance is 90 per cent frustration, and I think there's a lot in this. The plot of a romance is almost entirely driven by the frustration of the hero and heroine – the exasperation, the anxiety, the suspense of a relationship that isn't yet going right. Does he, doesn't he, will she, won't she...

Often, the storyline will involve some other conflict, a clash of ideas that keeps the two from getting together. Let's think about a specific plot, just off the top of our heads. *He* happens to spot something that tells him a particular field is probably the site of a Roman villa, and wants to start an archaeological dig. *She* wants the site's beauty left unmarred, and what's more it's the home of a rare orchid. Both have a point of view of great importance to them, and which will find sympathy with the reader. It's a conflict that's hard to resolve, and until they can agree they will never be able to give rein to the powerful attraction between them – a truly frustrating situation.

It's frustrating for the author too. How *do* you resolve such a situation? But the difficulties of doing so will result in a stronger story. If it's too easy, there'll be no satisfaction for the reader. It's got to be worked through to a real, feasible conclusion, and along the way you can have a lot of fun with all the kinds of things that happen in such situations. She can whip up local feeling, lead protests, organise a 'sit-in' on the day of the dig. He can try to persuade, cajole, lose his temper – but never bully. You want the reader to love this man, even if she's on the side of the heroine. And she wants the heroine to love him too.

All the time, we are aware of the powerful attraction between them. In different circumstances, they would love each other. It's such a shame that all these other conflicts are getting in the way. The reader is frustrated – but enjoyably so. She knows that it will all turn out all right, because this is a romance, so she doesn't have to worry about a possibly tragic ending. She keeps reading to find out just how it will happen. How will they resolve their differences and be able to get on with being in love?

The important point here is that the conflict is real. It isn't all based on a silly misunderstanding. Trivial conflicts frustrate the reader in an entirely different and not at all enjoyable way. Why doesn't the heroine just *say* she never received the letter? Why doesn't the hero swallow his stupid pride and apologise? If there are good, solid reasons, fine, but if the situation is trivial the reader will be irritated and probably not even bother to finish the book.

Sometimes the conflict is based on something that happened in the past. Perhaps the two had a relationship before. Perhaps they were engaged – even married – and something happened to break them up. Now they've met again and the old wounds are reopened – but the attraction is still there and so, deep down, is the love.

A lot depends on this 'back-story'. Why did they break up? How long ago was it? How did they both feel, and what's happened since? They won't have lived in a vacuum and there must be a new focus for conflict as well as the old one. There might have been other relationships, and one – or both – of these might be still in progress when they meet again, creating an interesting triangle – or quartet. But you must be able to resolve the original conflict as well as the one that starts with the present-day story.

The suspense of any story rests upon the tension between the characters – the frustrations they experience. And the strongest of these is sexual frustration. This is what makes the story a romance.

## Romance and sex

Sex is an important, not to say vital, ingredient in a story of romance. The glitzy sex-and-shopping novels that were popular a few years back were not, to my mind, 'romances' in this sense, for so often the sex was not shown as of a loving relationship. For true romance, there must be love, or at least the promise of it, rather than mere sexual gratification.

Sex comes into any novel that has an element of romance in it. Sex is the physical expression, of love between a man and a woman. A kiss, exchanged as such an expression, is a sexual kiss. The desire to express love in such a way is sex. If you want to write romance, it is no use trying to pretend it is all pure and platonic. Pure it may be – there's nothing impure about sex between loving partners – but it's not platonic. That's not the point of it at all, and make no mistake about it, as soon as they can those two are going to get between the sheets and do what comes naturally. They're human beings, aren't they? Well, they should be, if you've been following my advice so far.

This doesn't mean the sexual element has to be explicitly described. There are still a number of authors who write successful romances that never go beyond a kiss, and even that isn't described in anatomical detail. But the tensions and frustrations are still there. The story wouldn't hold up if they were not. Good as the storyline might be, without that sexual element – the element of romance – the book would seem unfinished and unsatisfying.

To return to our imagined scenario, suppose the couple resolved their conflict over the archaeological dig without ever feeling and fighting any attraction between them. However interesting the details you may relate about rare orchids, Roman mosaic pavements and the painstaking methods of conducting an archaeological investigation, without emotion it will read like the minutes of a particularly dry meeting.

Emotions bring life to the story and the story to life. The emotion of the hero, who is truly excited by ancient Roman remains; the heroine, who is passionate about orchids. And then the totally unexpected emotion that flares up between them, the recognition of a soulmate and the despair of not being able to acknowledge this – which translates itself swiftly into an equally passionate antipathy.

The most powerful of these emotions is the sexual one. It is the driving force of humanity. It is the driving force of your story.

First and foremost, your story is about two people who fall in love. *Two* people – not just the heroine. Even though the story is, in most cases, told through her eyes, we must never forget that the hero has emotions too.

Jean Saunders (author of *Black Maddie, All in the April Morning,* etc.), who also writes as Sally Blake, Jean Innes and Rowena Summers says: 'One of the things that writers of romantic novels should keep in mind is that the hero is falling in love as well as the heroine. In many manuscripts that are destined to remain unpublished, all too often the arrogant (and so outdated) hero has been hateful to the heroine all the way through, and suddenly confesses his love for her on the last page. This is neither feasible nor acceptable to today's readers. The characters each author creates will dictate whether that particular novel is gentle or steamy, but no matter what the obstacles, their love scenes should portray the growing awareness and sexual tension between them. This is the very essence of the romantic genre.'

So, what about sex?

No, that's not an invitation. But let's look at the whole range of sex, as it is shown in the romance and romantic novel.

Anyone who has read any of these books at all will know that, as in all other forms of story-telling, the degree to which sex is portrayed has changed considerably over the past few years. Twenty years ago, in a Mills & Boon romance, we followed the loving couple to the bedroom door, only to have it closed firmly in our face. Now, not only do we go all the way with them in the bedroom, we often find that they don't wait to get there. Sex can take place almost anywhere – in a parked car, the middle of a field, a wood, on the side of a mountain... Just like real life.

Nor does the heroine always have a wedding ring on her finger. I remember the debates a few years ago about whether sex (in the story) should be permitted before marriage. After much agonising, it was finally admitted that since it did happen in real life – and not just secretly, since more and more couples were living together – it was starting to look unrealistically old-fashioned and prim to forbid it in stories that were supposed to be about 'today'. But, we were told sternly when we sent in our new, liberated manuscripts, there must still be 'commitment'. The hero should not get the heroine into bed (or the other way about) without there being a definite sense of commitment on both sides.

This sense of commitment was sometimes rather tenuous, and often amounted to no more than a feeling on the heroine's part that she would never love anyone but *him*. (Sometimes, this was used as a device to keep them apart, since she could not allow herself to fall in love, knowing the pain it would bring...) But since we knew they would end up with wedding bells even the faintest promise of commitment was enough, and moral obligation fulfilled.

Don't laugh too hard. I think that sense of commitment is an important factor. Romance itself depends upon it. When we're in love, we do feel committed to our lover. That's why we feel insecure if he's not equally committed, jealous if he seems to be paying attention to someone else. We want to show our love, and we want it returned. And for many women, it is only possible to contemplate or enjoy sex with a man for whom we feel that commitment.

I speak only for the woman here. I don't think it is quite the same for most men. Many men do feel there is a difference between the desire they feel for sex in itself and the desire they feel for sex with the woman they love. This is the root of statements like: 'It didn't mean a thing, darling, it's you I love'. In his terms, it's true, but how difficult it is for women to understand.

This purely biological response can be used – and indeed has been for years. It used to be referred to, delicately, as 'a man's needs'. The implication often was that a woman was in the wrong for denying man his needs, but liberation has released us from this particular guilt-trip and women no longer have to feel responsible for a man's biological problems.

We can still use this factor, though, in allowing the hero to be attracted to the heroine without actually having fallen in love with her – or without realising that this is really what's happened. For a long time, he can attribute his confusion to the fact that she's physically very desirable, while mentally he thinks she's on another planet. Being a man, he won't think about emotions at this stage, but a truly romantic man shouldn't take too long to get around to this. As Jean Saunders says, the arrogant male is outdated. The hero might not be entirely New Man, staying home to look after the kids while Mum has a career, but he will be much more sensitive than in the past.

He will also be committed, and he will not be a bully. He will not make love to the heroine to 'punish' her. He will not use brute strength to dominate her. He will be capable of tenderness as well as passion. He will, in short, be the man we would all like to fall in love with and would want to love us back. As the author, we want the reader to fall in love with him, and to achieve this we must feel this emotion ourselves – we must fall in love with him too.

Sometimes authors do this so successfully that they feel real pain when they finish a book. A danger is that when they start a new book, the same hero will appear again, albeit disguised with auburn hair instead of black. After a couple of books, the reader will get wise to this and reject the author's books, because however hard the reader herself fell for this man she doesn't want him served up again and again with different hair. She wants a new man to fall in love with.

So don't get lazy with your characters. Think about those backgrounds, the upbringing and the experiences that will have shaped them into different people. These are what make them live. And living characters make the story – they make it happen their way, which may not be necessarily the way you'd thought of in the first place.

Sex, then, is dealt with more realistically today in that we acknowledge that it happens and that is is a vital part of the story. How far we go in describing it depends upon our own style, and the story itself.

Some writers never describe anything more than a kiss, and they don't go too far with that. You will never be told about tongues and thighs. The sexual tension is supplied entirely by conveying the emotion felt by the characters. These are known as 'gentle' romances, but this does not mean that the storyline itself is weak in any way.

Others are 'steamy'. Every encounter is drawn in graphic detail. We're there in the bedroom – probably tucked up in bed – with the lovers, sharing every intimate moment. No holds are barred. A love scene can go on for several pages and at the end of it the reader feels almost as exhausted (pleasurably, we hope) as the characters.

There is a place for both of these extremes and all stops in between. Some readers find steaminess too strong, others enjoy it and search the pages for an example before they decide to buy the book. And why not? Sex is a normal, everyday occurrence, part of life and, since it's undoubtedly the driving force behind our books, there's no reason why it shouldn't be fully incorporated in our story.

It depends entirely on you and the readers you appeal to. Some writers have a picture in their minds of the reader for whom they are writing their books. A little old lady with a bundle of knitting, a thirty-something career woman, a lively young university student. Others just write the story without thinking too much about who is going to read it. Each will gradually find their own public.

And the reader may not be quite what you think. The little old lady might have a dozen children – and she might spend all her time knitting for them now, but never forget that she's had a lifetime's experience of sex. A lot more than the bright young student. There's no reason why she shouldn't enjoy reading about it.

I also think there is another case for writing quite explicitly about sex. Romantic novels are read by young girls as well as mature women and old ladies. Many of them are totally inexperienced, and none of them can have had all that much. We hear a lot about sex education in schools, and how youngsters today know far, far more than we did – but do they really?

Do they really know how it feels to be loved, tenderly and passion-ately, by a man they are in love with? And how it feels to love him back? Do they understand the feelings that go beyond mere sensu-ality, and keep a couple together through all kinds of vicissitudes, some almost too great to be borne? Are they told this in sex education classes or behind the bike sheds? Are they told it *anywhere* but in fiction? In a romantic novel?

Write whatever you believe in. Your editor will soon tell you if it's too strong – or not strong enough. She is the person most in touch with what readers want and while a good editor won't force you into a mould that doesn't fit, she can steer you in the right direction.

Whatever level you find, it will be right for some readers and the size of the romance-reading public is such that the number will be consid-erable. But it is true to say that sex does sell. People like reading about it. You don't have to include love scenes that are out of place in the story – they must happen naturally as a result of the characters' emotions and actions – but if they do happen (and it's difficult to envisage a romance without love scenes) then they may as well be described in whatever detail you yourself think appropriate. You would describe a meal, a room, a garden if it had a place in the story. You'd give every word of a furious argument. Why stop at the very heart of the story, the essence of what it's all about?

But how do you write a love scene that doesn't end up as soft porn? Where's the difference?

The vital thing to remember is that a love scene is *emotional*. It is filled with the most intense emotions most of us will ever experience. Generally, in a romance, the scene will be described through the heroine's eyes. She is the one feeling the emotions with which the reader wants to identify. Talk about her emotions rather than the clinical aspects of lovemaking.

What does she feel as the hero kisses her, as his lips move slowly, tenderly, over hers, as his fingertips caress her breasts? Use of language is important here. The words that convey what a woman wants from sex – tender, caress, fingertips – all implying a loving relationship rather than a merely sexual one. It is the content of emotion, of deep, loving desire, that turns a passage that might otherwise be coldly pornographic into something that is warm, exciting and romantic.

If the emotion is there, you can be as explicit as you like – or as your editor will allow you. Or you can convey as much spine-tingling eroticism in no more than a single kiss. It all depends on what the heroine (usually) feels about it. And what you yourself feel, too. It is her passion that is being transmitted to the reader, with you as the transmitter.

Generally, the more clinical a description becomes, the less passionate and tender it will be, and the less romantic. People speak of the 'mystery' of sex, and perhaps it is to preserve this mystery that some of us like to have the lights off, or close our eyes at the most intimate moments. There is a crudity about too blunt a description that kills the romance. Again, use of language is all-important.

I am perfectly happy to describe the act of making love, making it quite clear what is happening – but I don't use crude or taboo words either for lovemaking or for body parts. For me, this demeans the whole process. Nor do I use the proper, rather clinical, words for the most intimate organs, not because I am afraid to use them but because these are not (yet) used in ordinary conversation. They are not 'romantic'.

Silly euphemisms and baby-talk aren't the answer either. But do we need to refer quite so explicitly? We describe other activities without having to mention every tiny detail – for instance, we know that if someone catches something thrown to them, they've used their hands. We know how food is eaten without describing every bite. In the same way, often all we need do is say what the hero and heroine are doing and *what they are feeling about it*, and the reader will know how they're doing it!

This has the advantage of letting the reader do some of the work – and allowing it to be pleasurable work. The joy of reading fiction lies in the imaginative process that the writer unlocks in the reader's mind. It is the skill of a writer who can unlock imagination that the reader didn't even know she had, that makes readers go back to her books time and time again, and makes them eagerly await each new one she writes.

Sex may be treated a little differently in the romantic novel. Here, we have a number of different viewpoint characters, and some of them are almost certainly going to be men. You may want to write about love scenes between more than one couple, and these will involve greater or lesser degrees of real love; some of them may not involve love at all, nor any kind of affection.

Because the romantic novel has a wider scope, these subjects can be dealt with alongside the true love story that must be the main thread of the story. The main heroine herself may be involved in scenes of loveless sex – a rape, for instance, or the sexual acts of a loveless marriage. Clearly, her emotions are going to be very different, but they are still the driving force of the episode and must be treated with as much sensitivity.

Scenes between couples who have no love for each other and are looking only for sexual gratification are different. If there is truly no emotion involved, the very coldness of the transaction will come across in the description. Be certain that this in itself is the purpose of your including such a scene and adds value to the story; otherwise you risk boring your reader, or creating distaste rather than interest. Or you may be guilty of gratuitous titillation, which is approaching soft porn.

When we look more closely at a scene of this sort, we will see that there is indeed emotion there, however well hidden. The two people involved have a reason for sharing sex. At least one of them must be an important character in the story, or we wouldn't be seeing his (or her) viewpoint. If the scene is important to the story, the reason must be emotional.

Let's take as an example, a man who goes to a prostitute – the most loveless voluntary sexual encounter of all. If he is your viewpoint character, and the prostitute will take no further part in the story, his reason for using her must be an important factor in the story.

Why does he do this? Is he so inadequate that this is his only way of getting sexual release? Has he been parted from his real lover for so long that frustration drives him into another – any – woman's arms. Is it his first time, a bid to lose his virginity? All these are emotional reasons that may be important to the story, and validate the scene's inclusion. These emotions are the ones the reader needs to understand.

What about the prostitute? If she is your character, we need to know her reasons for taking to this way of life. Perhaps she's been forced into it by poverty; perhaps she's under the domination of a pimp. Perhaps she's the 'tart with a heart' – shamelessly sexy, happy with her way of life (or is she?) and full of warmth and compassion. Her emotions bring her to life.

And this particular scene must be important – either to illustrate all this, or to show her at a crossroads.

In *Bid Time Return*, I had a couple marry thinking they were in love. But they had totally different expectations and these became horribly clear on their wedding night.

Louisa, the young Victorian girl, had been brought up without any knowledge or education of sex. (And she hadn't had any romantic novels to read, either.) She had no idea what to expect. She knew nothing of anatomy. When she saw what was happening to her husband, she was appalled; she thought he was deformed. The consummation of the marriage hurt and terrified her and when Nicholas fell asleep, she thought he had died.

There was nothing improbable about this. I have heard elderly women today say that this was just their experience. Young women were told nothing. They were left to find out on their wedding night.

In this story, I wanted to show what the man was feeling, so I told this scene through Nicholas's eyes as well, though in his case it was through his thoughts afterwards. He had no idea that Louisa was suffering. He thought her cries and struggles were part of the flirtatious behaviour she had indulged in earlier. Carried away by his own desire, he believed that she was as happy as he. He never understood what had gone wrong between them.

This was the story of a disastrous relationship, and there was no love in the sexual act after this. But there was a great deal of emotion, and it was essential to describe it in some detail.

If the couple are both simply out for sex – a young woman of today who carries condoms in her handbag, and a man who will quite naturally take advantage of her willingness – you will still need to involve the emotions of your main character (and both may be viewpoint characters at some point in the story). You may want to explore what happens, emotionally, to a young woman who treats sex in a way that has until recently been associated more with young men. This might even be the theme of your novel, seeing what happens when she actually falls in love. There's nothing really new about it. Look at some of the classical heroines – Moll Flanders, Becky Sharpe.

Sexually, there really is nothing new under the sun. But if you are writing either a romance or a romantic novel, you must never forget the tenderness, the sensitivity, the passion. These are the essential ingredients, and they can all be encapsulated in that one, vital word: emotion.

# **Summary**

- Romance is 90 per cent frustration.

- Your reader must identify with the heroine – and fall in love with the hero.

- There must be strong sexual attraction – but it doesn't have to be explicit.

- Never forget the emotion.

# 10
# HISTORY AND RESEARCH

## When did it happen?

Both romances and romantic novels can be written about any period in history, from Stone Age times to the present day. Admittedly, a modern-day story is likely to be more appealing than one set in the days of the caveman, but there are plenty of historical periods in between that you can use. In this though, as with everything else, fashions change, and it's as well to be aware of what is popular and what isn't.

People have been saying for some years now that the day of the historical novel is over. Perhaps it is true that the golden age is past, but there are still plenty of historical novels being published and plenty of readers out there who want them. So, if that's what you really want to write, don't let current thought put you off. In my opinion, the historical novel is likely to return, especially as a result of all the costume dramas recently presented on TV.

What's more, 'history' is getting longer. The Second World War is now defined as history, and pretty soon the fifties and then the sixties will join it. These periods are immensely popular now and likely to go on being so. It's all a matter of perception.

Within the genre of the historical novel, fashions come and go. The Regency novel was big a few years ago; the gothic novel came and went, almost entirely with Victoria Holt; Victorian settings have held strong for the past few years. Cavalier times seem out of favour, and not many writers can deal with medieval times with the expertise of Ellis Peters (aka Edith Pargeter) and Norah Lofts. But the success of Ellis Peters with her Brother Cadfael novels – which are surely romantic novels as well as detective stories – proves that if you can write well enough, you can choose your own period.

Indeed, it's not a good idea to take too much notice of what's in fashion now. It's two years ahead you should be thinking of – because that's roughly the time it will take you to research and write your book and then get it through the publishing process, if you are lucky enough to find a publisher first time out. So don't jump on to any bandwagon that's been rolling for too long. It's likely to be coming to a halt pretty soon.

Generally, the same principle applies to choosing a period as to any other aspect of your writing. You will always do better with a subject that you find interesting. If you have no rapport with the Victorians, you won't be able to write a novel set during their period. Pick a time in which you are interested, for which you feel sympathy. Remember, you are going to have to do a lot of research, and if it makes you yawn, your reader is going to be even more bored.

To me, one of the most interesting periods of history is the nineteenth century. So much happened then. There were huge technological advances, giant leaps forward in industry, bringing all the conflicts that such progress causes. There were social changes too: the rise of the trades unions, the first steps towards universal suffrage, the beginning of education for the masses, the birth of the feminist movement. In all sorts of ways, it was a time like no other, and we are still living with its effects.

I cannot believe that sex has always been treated as primly as we are led to believe the Victorians treated it (and I suspect that much of that is a myth). Look at the bawdiness of Shakespeare, of Chaucer, of Defoe. And it wasn't just sex. Women were freer in the seventeenth and eighteenth centuries. Something happened during the Victorian age to make it different, and we tend to think it was ever thus. It wasn't.

All those changes that were taking place make it possible to include a wide canvas of events in a story. That's partly why the Victorian period is such a rich vein for writers to tap. Another reason is that it is still not very distant from us. The Victorians have left legacies that we see around us every day. Many of us live in Victorian houses or work in Victorian buildings, and it is currently fashionable to decorate our houses in keeping with the period. The railways began then. There is an enormous amount of Victorian furniture and paraphernalia to collect. For the older generation, there are family members – parents and grandparents – who were the last of the Victorians, brought up by parents who were themselves very firmly Victorians.

The industrial revolution brought scientists and engineers with whom we can still identify. Steam power, the great invention of the eighteenth century, was in its heyday in Victorian times, and there is still great nostalgia for steam. The political and social changes set the scene for our political system today.

Victorian novels, combining at their best the gothic romance of the Brontës and the grittiness of Dickens, have been popular for years, and even though their popularity has dwindled a little (partly, I suspect, because there are just so many of them on the shelves now) I don't think they will ever fade completely. There will always be room for one more.

The Regency period is another that has enjoyed great favour, with Georgette Heyer as the doyenne of them all. Regency novels are romances rather than romantic novels. They, possibly more than any other, follow strict guidelines. The Regency period was a short but merry one – for some people. Life was all Mayfair and Bath, ballgowns and duels – for some people. And these people, the 'beautiful people' of the time, are the only ones who figure in such novels. The Regency novel does not look at the poverty, the squalor, as the Victorian novel usually does. Like the characters who figure in its pages, it behaves as if such things do not exist.

I am not condemning the Regency novel for this. I think it is probably a fairly faithful representation of life as it was for a section of society, and it has its stories to be told and enjoyed. Why not? It's the same kind of escapist relaxation as the contemporary romance. But remember, if this is what you want to write, that your readers will not thank you for bringing reality of a different sort into the story. Like the readers of the contemporary romance, they want to wallow for a while in a land where the worst that could happen to a man was to lose all he owned at cards or to meet his rival at dawn with pistols for two. And it won't be the hero who falls, clutching his heart, or is thrown off the family estate. If it is, the story will probably be about how he regains his rightful possessions.

If you change the format, you are moving into the realm of the romantic novel, and different rules apply. Always make sure you know what the difference is, and don't take the risk of falling between two stools.

# Family sagas and regional novels

Many Victorian novels come into the category of 'family saga'. The 'trouble at mill' stories are almost all of this type. They give the writer a good, solid background to work from, with plenty of characters – the Victorians were very obliging in producing big families – and strong, emerging industrial backgrounds with lots of conflict. If you can find an unusual industry, that nobody else has tackled, so much the better.

This kind of story will also invariably be a regional novel. Industry always has been peculiar to certain areas of the country, for reasons ranging from the presence of coalfields to a good harbour – in other words, materials and communications. Landscape too, then, will feature in the story, and you will have an extra richness from the people who live there. A sense of place is vital to these stories. The background is very strong and you will need to research thoroughly.

Family stories have their own rules. Try not to involve too big a family – a large crowd of characters can get unwieldy and confusing for the reader, and you may not have space to give them all proper attention. The length of a family saga is usually around 120,000–160,000 words. Although this may seem dauntingly long, if you are going to tell the stories of, say, four or five main viewpoint characters with one predominating, the word count for each one is quite low. It isn't calculated quite so unfeelingly as that (not by me, anyway) but it's a rough guide to the way such a story will work out.

Even before Victorian times, people had large families. There weren't many ways of preventing it, other than the early death of a mother worn out by childbearing – see memorial tablets in churches for evidence of this – and high infant mortality rates. Fewer people reached adulthood, but still, quite a few did manage it. Even so, remember that almost every family would have been struck by the tragedy of bereavement and there might be large gaps between living siblings.

There are a number of ways of getting rid of unwanted family members. Don't kill them all off. You may need them later. Send them away some-where – on a crusade, to the colonies, to America or Australia as pioneers or black sheep. Girls can get married and go to live somewhere else in Britain, coming home only occasionally. There can be family quarrels. Or if the mother dies young, the father may not marry again.

If he does, we may get a replay of the Cinderella story, with step-children coming in to the picture and more new conflicts. More characters, too – with another family in the background. You see why you don't want to start off with too many!

A good rule to remember is always to keep the number of characters to a minimum. You will almost certainly find new characters creeping in during the writing, and these may even be new viewpoint characters, so try to keep the cast of thousands down to start with.

The family saga has the advantage that it can be told over several books, turning into a trilogy, a quartet or even more. Iris Gower wrote a series of six books about her 'Sweyn's Eye' in Wales and then went on to do even more in similar vein. Each book should stand alone, even if it is part of a series, but you still have the disadvantage that many people simply will not read any of them unless they can get them in the right order. In extreme cases, this can mean a reader never gained, which is a great shame. It needn't stop you writing them, but it's a point for you (and the publisher, who is well aware of this) to bear in mind.

The multiple-book saga can be approached in two ways. My own Glassmakers trilogy told the story of a family in three generations. The main characters of the first book, *Crystal*, were parents in *Black Cameo* and grandparents in *Chalice*, taking a less prominent part each time.

In *The Carpetmakers*, I used the same viewpoint character throughout. This made a big difference to the timespan. The Glassmakers, which told the stories of three generations, went right through Victoria's reign; *The Carpetmakers* took in less than forty years, starting with Rebecca's birth. The books themselves were about the same length, but the stories were different.

*An Endless Song* had an even shorter timespan. Rowenna was twenty years old when it started and only twenty-three at the end. Clearly, she had an eventful few years!

There are no hard-and-fast rules. Each story has its own timespan, and the length, or number of words, depends on the events within the story and your style in telling it. You have to decide how much of the story needs to be told to bring it to the best length for a book; if it is packed with incidents that need a lot of description, dialogue or action, it may need to be split into more than one book. Or you may have to forgo telling some and use it in a compressed form such as back-story or flashback.

Make sure that the reader knows in what period the story is set. Generally, it will be made clear as soon as possible just when the story happened. Try to convey this information in the first page or two, either by stating the date or tying the beginning to some event that every reader will recognise – the year of Queen Victoria's death, for instance, or Caesar's invasion of Britain. If it's contemporary there is often no need to tie it to a particular year – indeed, it can be a disadvantage to do so, since it can 'date' the story unwelcomingly – but you do need to have a time in your mind, so that you don't commit any anachronisms.

This is more of a danger in period or historical writing. Some books, particularly gothic novels, are delightfully vague about exactly when they took place. You know it is probably late nineteenth century because they are travelling by train as well as being met in governess carts, and because of the clothes they wear. Apart from that, no hint is given. Nor need there be. These stories are not concerned with national politics or whatever technological advances were being made (apart from the odd penny-farthing bicycle or new motorcar). But the writer must have more than a vague idea. You must know whether it was likely for the heroine to travel in a governess cart or a phaeton. What *was* a phaeton? And what was it like to travel by train then? Did carriages have corridors? Even if you're not going to use all the facts you discover, you need to have a good assortment to pick from, to give those little touches of authenticity.

# **Research**

Research is not confined to historical novels. You often need to do just as much for contemporary writing. It is a necessary and time-consuming part of writing, and most writers, because we are an insatiably curious breed, find it a fascinating process – remember, we always try to write about the things that interest us, so it will be rewarding to investigate these subjects further. But sometimes you will have to research subjects that are less interesting to you, because your book demands them. Don't gloss over these subjects. You may even find that research awakens an interest.

Many writers find that the research becomes so absorbing that they have difficulty in deciding when they have done enough and should start writing. I don't have this problem, because I am invariably eager to get on with the book, but I can see that the natural researcher or historian is likely to become immersed. I can only say that you will have to evolve your own discipline. And a contract with a deadline concentrates the mind wonderfully.

Research can be undertaken in a number of different ways. For a contemporary romance that involves a profession or hobby you know nothing about, you need to find someone who is an expert. For my ballooning book, *Sky High*, I went to balloon manufacturer Don Cameron. I attended a ballooning weekend during which he gave lectures and showed films as well as taking the group on a flight (magical), and he kindly talked to me separately and then read my manuscript and corrected any points I had inadvertently got wrong – for instance, I had included a balloon that was used for advertising cigarettes. 'No cigs!' he wrote in the margin.

This is one of the most 'fun' kinds of research, and can add immeasurably to your own life. I have also learnt to canoe and ski, both of which made good backgrounds for romances. Of course, if you are already expert at something, you have a head start.

For industrial backgrounds, you can go to the industry itself. Most have their own archives or historian, or there will be someone who has made themselves an expert. For the Glassmakers trilogy, I went to Stuart Crystal in Stourbridge, and spent many hours watching the glassmaking process and talking to the glassmakers. I was very fortunate in that glass was being made in exactly the same way, with the same tools, as in Victorian times, so I could see precisely what my own characters would have been doing. I was also supplied with photocopies of the glassmakers' own journal of the time, which gave me information on the development of the trade itself, the growth of the trades unions and so on.

Because these were regional novels, I also had to research into the area. The best way to do this, of course, is to visit it. Go to the main library and look in the reference section for local books. Then you will know which ones to apply for through the library service. If you can't borrow these and they're unobtainable in the shops, you may be able to arrange for them to be sent to your own local library so that you can study them there.

I always go to local bookshops as well and buy books from their local interest shelves. Many are written and published by local historians and societies, and unobtainable anywhere else, and these are often the most valuable. If there is an industry that is special to the area in which you have located your story, you more are likely to find such books, written by enthusiasts and experts.

Local newspapers are another good source. Many of them are now on microfiche and you can see them in your local library and photocopy the sections you want. National newspaper and magazine archives are also available for researchers. And there are now a number of 'nostalgia' publications – magazines, books and anthologies devoted to the past. And don't forget videos of old news programmes and Pathe Pictorial cinema news.

Old maps, too, are invaluable for the historical novelist. The Ordnance Survey publish facsimile versions of their original 1-inch maps, which will show you just what it was like in your area. And I was delighted to discover a reprint of the Victorian London A–Z, which is wonderful for seeing exactly where your characters could have gone a hundred years ago.

In the same way, when researching in Corning, the small American town where I set *Chalice*, I was lent an old street directory that sat beside me all through the writing of the book. I had been to Corning and arranged to visit the glassworks and museum there – well worth a visit if you're in the area – and had several sessions with a delightful and charming local historian who pointed me in the direction of a number of other books that were invaluable, including his own massive *History of Corning* which became my bible.

There are also a number of books now published in the Chronicle series – *Chronicle of the 20th Century, Chronicle of the Second World War*, etc. These are huge tomes that take a day by day look at events that happened, reporting them as if in a daily newspaper. They are tremendously useful, but use them with care. Some of the events are known only with hindsight, and the information would not have been available to the public at the time – this applies especially to wartime chronicles. This doesn't matter if you are using the information as part of your background, where it is appropriate, but it does if you are writing through the viewpoint of a character who would not have possessed this information.

I have already mentioned oral history tapes, which are held in some libraries. These are accounts spoken by elderly people, and sometimes their memories go back a very long way and include memories recounted to them by their parents and grandparents – in this way, you can hark back for as much as a hundred and fifty years. Take care though – these memories may very well be distorted by time!

There are also county record offices and collections held by archaeological and local history societies, some of them quite extensive. And of course, there is the General Register Office where records are held of all births, marriages and deaths in England and Wales since 1 July 1837. Equally useful is the Census Room of the Public Record Office in Portugal Street, where records have been kept since 1841 (earlier if you don't need names).

Sometimes you must be prepared to travel. I decided that I simply *had* to go to Paris to research *Black Cameo*. Much of this book was set in a French glassmaker's family. I spent an awesome day in the wonderful showrooms and museum of Baccarat and then browsed among all the other glassmakers' showrooms in Rue de Paradis, entranced by the glittering displays. At the same time, I needed to research the Franco-Prussian War and the Siege of Paris, since the timing of my story made it necessary to include this, and lo and behold, I discovered that balloons played quite a large part in this war. So two of my interests came together.

Balloons were used to get information out of Paris to the government, then seated in Bordeaux, and orders back in. I could write another book about this fascinating process – and you will find quite a lot in *Black Cameo* – but basically the idea was to take large numbers of carrier pigeons out by balloon and then fly them back covered in messages – not only tied to their legs, but even painted on their feathers! Obviously this was going to make a colourful episode in the book, especially as my primary purpose in using the balloons was to get my hero out of Paris, so I had to research it thoroughly.

Reading novels written at the time is another way of doing research – not to plagiarise, but to discover useful information about what was happening, and how people talked and behaved. For *Black Cameo*, I read Zola's *Debacle* and gained some good background colour, and I also read Arnold Bennett's *The Old Wives' Tale* – and discovered something else.

*The Old Wives' Tale* contains several chapters about the Siege of Paris and the involvement of balloons. I had read this some time before, and I also read Alistair Horne's *The Fall of Paris*, which gave me yet more information about this time.

Finding out where the information about balloons might be held wasn't easy but eventually I discovered that there was a whole floor devoted to ballooning at the Musée de la Poste in Montparnasse. Here, I found rooms full of fascinating displays and information, including an archive room filled with magazines, newspapers and other material devoted to this period. And in one of the magazines was a series of eye-witness accounts of the balloons and their adventures. I photocopied these and took them home with me.

It was when I was translating them, in the laborious schoolgirl French that somehow managed to get me all over Paris, that I became aware of a sense of déjà vu. Somewhere, I'd read them before. And then the penny dropped.

I got out *The Old Wives' Tale* and there it was – almost word for word, the same description. Bennett had been there first. He must have read exactly these accounts, taken them home and translated them just as I had.

I still used the episode and because it was a true account there are inevitable similarities. But I hope that not too many readers will think I cribbed the scene from Bennett. It confirmed for me the foolishness of using words that someone else has already written, however obscure the source might seem. There may be someone else who has seen them first – and that someone may be more famous than you!

Research may involve spending hours in museums and libraries, digging out obscure material and studying it. It may be very specialised. It may involve translating material from foreign languages, ancient Latin or Middle English. If you're an expert in this field, fine, but what if you're not?

There are researchers who make a living from doing this. They advertise in writing magazines and *The Author*, the organ for members of the Society of Authors. They will undertake to do what- ever research you may need. Whether they justify their cost is for you to decide, since you must set it against the money you hope eventually to make from the book. In terms of time, travel and accommodation, they may well prove cost-effective.

If you do employ a researcher, make sure he or she understands what it is you want, and more importantly, is in sympathy with the kind of material you yourself would pick out. For my Second World War books, I did the research myself until it came to the last one, and a friend offered to help. He took on the task with huge enthusiasm, going off to the city library day after day, working his way steadily through the local newspapers for the last two years of the war and noting down 'snippets' that he thought I'd find interesting.

He did a marvellous job. But suppose he hadn't had a rapport with my ideas. Suppose, instead of the human stories he picked up, I'd found myself with a pile of expensive photocopies of maps of the battlefields of Europe or technical details of the war at sea – neither of which would have been of any use to me at all? Briefing your researcher properly is essential.

Finding out when actual events took place can sometimes be difficult. Not only do you need to discover whether the first of May in a particular year was a Tuesday, you must remember the ten-day change from the Julian to the Gregorian calendar in 1582; furthermore, some countries didn't adopt the new calendar until quite recently (Greece was last, in 1923). When it comes to finding out, for instance, the date of Easter you can find yourself in a real quandary. Saints' days and religious festivals provide more traps for the unwary. You may not think it matters, and indeed it is often possible to gloss over these facts so that it isn't necessary to tie in quite so tightly. But to me there is a satisfaction about knowing that all these small details are accurate. And it's nice to know that if there is an expert out there, reading your book, he will pounce on that little fact and say 'Yes! That's right! This writer knows her stuff', rather than shaking his head in disgust and throwing the book aside.

I like to include things that really did happen. It gives me a good feeling to know that bandleader Joe Loss was at South Parade Pier in Southsea on a particular date during the war, that Arthur Askey was at the King's Theatre, that my characters could have been there and that some of my readers might have been too. And it gives the reader a good feeling too. She will say either 'That's right – *I* was there that night. That's how it was,' and feel even more a part of the story; or she will subconsciously recognise the authenticity and say 'That's how it *must* have been' and feel a stronger belief in what you are telling her.

Events like this are easy to discover through the newspaper archives. But dates and events further back may be less easy. Fortunately, there are books to help us with this, and two that can be recommended are *The Handbook of Dates for Students of English History*, and *British Calendar Customs*, published by the Folklore Society.

Weather too can trip you up. It's sometimes important, and invariably adds to the authentic feel of the book, to know whether there was a particularly hard winter or poor summer in a particular year. For instance, there were a number of desperately cold summers during the early Middle Ages (now thought to be the result of volcanic activity elsewhere in the world) and almost no harvests were gathered during those years. You could not  write convincingly of that period if you didn't know this. There are a number of books about weather, and a general reading of history around your particular dates will help too.

Think about other aspects of historical living as well. Judy Saxton (author of *Still Waters, Harvest Moon*, etc.) immerses herself in her background, getting to know it really well. 'I keep an eye on slang and fashion so that, although I don't hit the reader over the head with '20s headbands or '40s New Look, I see my characters in the right sort of clothing, which helps create atmosphere.'

Money, clothes, furniture, transport – all these were different. You don't always need to go too deeply into these – just enough to create atmosphere is sufficient – but you do need to be aware of the possibility of pitfalls. And it helps to know that there are ways of finding these things out.

One of my most useful reference books is the *Shell Book of Firsts*. This tells you about the 'first' of a wide range of subjects, from the first safety-pin, the first woman dentist and the first newspaper cartoon, to the first water closet, the first box of chocolates and the first 'steamship successfully fitted with screw propellers'. Don't laugh. You could need any one of them.

Another useful reference is the *Guinness Book of Answers*, which is a general compendium of information on such subjects as meteorology, the sciences, philosophy, engineering and sport. I would not be without either of these two books.

It is impossible to stress too highly the value of thorough research. I have had a number of letters about my books, and every one of them remarks upon the authenticity and the believability – letters from glassmakers or the sons and daughters of glassmakers; letters from people who experienced the war at far closer hand than I did; letters from people who knew the iron-mining industry in Furness, and a letter from a man who started off by saying 'I have just read your book about glassmaking and I don't know how you could have done it!'

My heart sank when I read those words. It sounded like an accusation. But he went on to say that he could not understand how I, a woman, could possibly have such insight and understanding of the glass trade. Women just hadn't figured in it. And yet somehow I'd got it right – even details he'd thought were trade secrets. I'd caught the atmosphere of the furnace room, the camaraderie and conflicts, the whole flavour of life within the glassmakers' families. He then went on to read some of my other books and write to me again, expressing further amazement. He was a man who had run his own glassmaking business, who had himself lived a life that would make a book.

What had convinced him? I think it was down to three things: the passion and imagination of which I have already spoken – the deep excitement and interest that I felt for glass and its manufacture; the imagination and insight I brought to the creation of the characters and their stories; and the attention to detail. I would never have caught and kept the attention of a man who was an expert in the field unless I had conducted my research thoroughly. He would never have gone on to read any of my other books. And who knows how many people he told, and how many new readers I gained through his enthusiasm?

Don't forget your characters in all this search for facts. Joanna Trollope, who never forgets hers for a moment, has this warning: 'Remember that your characters may well be *before* the theories of Sigmund Freud and will therefore ring much more truly if they are concerned with codes of conduct rather than with trips round their own psyches. Also, in my view, you can't do too much research, even for a modern novel, and you can't use too little of it in the novel afterwards...'

Research, then, is vital. And the good news is that it is easier today than it has ever been in the past. We have a new tool to help us, a tool such as has never been seen before, and one that deserves a chapter to itself. The Internet.

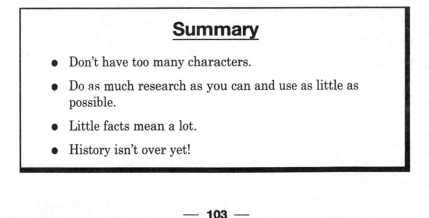

## Summary

- Don't have too many characters.
- Do as much research as you can and use as little as possible.
- Little facts mean a lot.
- History isn't over yet!

# 11

# THE INTERNET

Notice how I ended the last chapter on a cliff-hanger, so that you just had to turn the page to find out what happens next? Well, I hope you did anyway. Because the Internet is the most exciting new research tool to come on the scene since Caxton printed *The Recuyell of the Histories of Troye*. And it's definitely more advanced.

The Internet is so new that only a few authors have realised its potential, but it is rapidly becoming easier to use and will within the next few years become familiar to almost all of us. It will soon be incorporated into telephones and televisions and you may find yourself 'on-line' almost without knowing it.

The most important part of the Internet for the general user is the World Wide Web. Web is a good name for it, since its best analogy is that of a spider's web, with many different pathways linked to a central intelligence. This centre is a computer – or a number of computers, all over the world – and anyone with a computer, a modem and a subscription to a provider (another computer with direct access to this web) can link into the whole. The modem is not expensive and subscriptions are remarkably low-priced for such a comprehensive system – at the time of writing you need pay only ten or twelve pounds monthly. On top of this you pay for your telephone calls, but since these are charged at local rate only, this too is comparatively cheap. Some sources also demand a subscription but you may well decide that there is so much else available that you don't need them.

What happens is that the modem links your telephone and computer together, so that instead of calls coming through the receiver they are directed into your computer and arrive on the screen as text or pictures. Sound and video can be incorporated too, and great strides are being made in their presentation.

Once linked into the system you are free to browse or 'surf' the Net. You can use your computer as a search facility in a vast range of encyclopaedias, libraries, museums, archives, daily newspapers (on the day they are printed) and general information. The amount of information on the Web is almost incalculable and growing all the time. It is all there for you to discover.

The searching is done by means of 'search engines', which are in fact large computers that 'tour' the Web constantly looking for new references and adding them to their own vast repertoire. All you have to do is access one of these engines by typing in its name and address (for example www.yahoo) and the screen will show you a form to fill in. This is simplicity itself – all it asks is that you enter in key words that will give it a clue as to what you are looking for. This done, it will go off for a few moments and search, and then back it will come with a list of 'matches'. Scroll these down and pick out the one you think most appropriate, and you will find an entire document of anything from half a page to a hundred being downloaded into your machine. You can read it on screen or save it to disk and print it out to read later.

There are a few things to watch out for. It's very easy to stay on-line for hours at a time, fascinated by the sheer scale of information and the huge range of subjects available. Even at local rates, this can add up. You may be quite happy about this – it's cheaper than a night at the pub, and probably a lot cheaper than spending time and money in travel. It's also cheaper than a lot of long-distance telephone calls. But you don't *have* to spend this amount of money.

Once you've got the hang of it, you can very quickly judge what is most useful and save it to be printed out once you have switched off. You will also learn the key words that are most likely to bring the information you want. And there are now facilities that allow you to save documents before they are downloaded, so that a swift glance will tell you that these hundred pages are going to be worth having, and you can save the entire document with one click.

Here's an example of how this works. During the writing of my fourth 'Street At War' book, *Moonlight and Lovesongs*, I suddenly wanted information about the film *Casablanca*, including the words of the song 'As Time Goes By' and the name of its composer. As a sceptical friend pointed out, I could have gone to the local library and found a book about films. But that would have involved at least an hour's travel (I live in the country) plus the time taken to find the book (if they had it) and write down the information. It would also have cost me for petrol, parking etc.

Instead, I went on-line, tapped in the key words 'movie+Casablanca' and *within two minutes* of having first logged-on, I was holding in my hand a printout of several pages of text. I had pictures of the stars, the words of the song (and its composer's name) and the full review and story of the film as published in the *New York Times* when it was first released. I could have had even more, but this was enough. And all for the cost of a local phone call.

On another occasion, I wanted information about the American bomber the Flying Fortress. Again, within minutes I had everything I needed – things I didn't even *know* I needed but which gave more authenticity to my story. Quickly, cheaply and again without moving from my desk.

I was able to use it, too, to prove to my editor that my memory was correct as well as my research. I mentioned earlier that I had used an appearance by Joe Loss at Southsea during the Second World War. I referred to his signature tune 'In The Mood', and my editor came back with a puzzled 'But that was Glenn Miller's signature tune.' No, I said, it was Joe Loss's. 'But Glenn Miller *wrote* it,' she protested. I know, I said, but Joe Loss used it as his signature tune.

I was 99 per cent certain that I was right, but the one per cent kept me awake that night and I knew I would have to make sure. So, back to the Internet. And there it was. All I ever wanted to know about Joe Loss, including the all-important fact that he enjoyed such a success with Glenn Miller's 'In The Mood' that he used it as his signature tune for the next fifty years.

Information on the Internet is growing exponentially. By the time this book is published, there will be even more, and more of us will be using it. It is the most marvellous research facility that has ever been available and the writer who needs to research and yet shrugs it aside will, I am afraid, be shrugged aside in his own turn.

This isn't all the Internet can offer. Most of us now have heard of e-mail – the facility to communicate with others also on-line, without having to use the expensive national or international telephone. There is no need for both of you to be on-line at the same moment – you can simply leave your message to be picked up when your correspondent next logs on, and when you next do so you may find the response waiting for you. Or you can chat in 'real time', using the screen as a medium to type your messages rather than speaking on the phone. Again, much cheaper, and you don't even have to know the other party exists before you start; you find them through the subject you are concerned with. Or perhaps you've joined a newsgroup and posted a question; someone will come up with the answer and away you go. Again, a source of research that simply couldn't have existed before.

It isn't all 'historical' information. Look for a place – Vancouver, say – and you will find a plethora of documents to choose from, including such things as the bulletin board of the local sailing club, which will give you dates of their meetings, races, and so forth and a constantly updated weather forecast, with satellite photographs.

You can find information from all over the world – local government, businesses, schools, travel. You name it, it's likely to be there.

Once you are into your chosen subject, you can also leap across from document to document by using the 'hotlinks'. Again, it is easy. These show in blue, denoting further information available, and all you have to do is click; the new document will appear at once. You can wander for hours like this if you want to, and if you want to return to your original place, you can do so just as easily. You can even see where you've been – those items you looked at earlier are now pink. (This doesn't stop you looking at them again.)

By now, I hope that even the hardened sceptics amongst you will be able to understand not only the fascination of the Internet, but the sheer, down-to-earth practicality of it and its usefulness to authors.

Some authors even have their own pages on the Web, with information about themselves and their books. I do myself. Having your own Website is getting easier all the time and there is room for everyone. Because the Net isn't dependent on one central computer, the space available for knowledge and information is literally infinite – the term 'cyberspace' just had to be coined to describe it. This means that there is also a lot of rubbish out there, but you don't have to look at it, any more than you have to look at every book in a normal library. Nothing is forced upon you.

As you can see, I am a convert. And no, I don't have shares in the Internet. Nobody does. I don't spend hours surfing – I may even forget I've got it for days at a time. But when I want it, it's there – day or night. And when I ask it for information that might otherwise take me hours, days or even weeks to discover and cost me quite a lot of money in time and travel, it's invaluable.

## **Summary**

- Who's afraid of the World Wide Web?
- The Internet is the biggest encyclopaedia in existence.
- The Internet can save you time, travel and money.
- Promote yourself in cyberspace.

# 12

# SYNOPSES, DRAFTS
# AND BLURBS

> 'How do I write a synopsis?'
>
> 'How many drafts should I write?'
>
> 'What *is* a blurb? Do I really have to write it myself?'

These are questions that worry almost all new writers – they certainly worried me. But really there is no need to panic.

A synopsis is no more than the précis you probably learned to do at school. The number of drafts you write is up to you. And not all publishers ask you to write a blurb, but if yours does, just look at those on any book and follow suit.

## The synopsis

Basically, a synopsis is an outline of the story. You need to know how to write one because you will almost always be asked to provide one. Most publishers prefer to see a synopsis and a few chapters before agreeing to commission the book. This can be a help to the writer, since sometimes a commission can be obtained on the strength of a good synopsis, and if the publisher has any specific requirements, it is much easier to incorporate them at this stage.

A disadvantage can be that, once having started to write, you probably won't want to stop, and by the time the publisher has come back with a verdict you may have practically completed the book, only to discover that something completely different is required. In which case, you have three options. You can scrap what you've done and rewrite to the new requirements – which I would only do if there were a definite contract, since otherwise the publisher is under no obligation to accept your second effort even if you feel you've done everything you've been asked to do. You can send the book as you've written it, which rather negates the purpose of the synopsis in the first place, but if the publisher really likes your writing, you may prove that you were right all along. Or you can try another publisher.

You don't *have* to send in only a few chapters. You can always send the entire book. But it is *always* a good idea to send a synopsis.

So what should it include? Thinking of it as an outline clearly indicates that it needs to include all the salient points of the story. Characters, setting, period and plot. Don't be tempted to leave questions hanging enticingly in the air, leaving the editor in suspense – she doesn't want suspense at this stage. She wants to know that you can build the story to an exciting climax and bring it to a satisfying conclusion, and that this will stand up to a cold-blooded examination. Sometimes the difficulty a writer experiences in writing a synopsis stems from faults in the story, and if this is the case you should think again about your plot before even starting.

Do I hear cries of 'But suppose the story changes as I write? Didn't you say I ought to let the story develop in its own way?' Yes, I did, and stories often do change as they are written. Editors are quite used to that and if the final book is a success they won't object in the slightest. Nevertheless, the original synopsis must make sense. It is no use getting halfway through and then losing track, saying airily, 'It'll work itself out.' Your synopsis is your shop window, and it's got to be clear.

It doesn't have to be several pages long. Agent Caroline Sheldon recommends a single page; she says you ought to be able to get all relevant information in that space. I confess mine usually runs to two or three pages, but I would not write a synopsis longer than that. And this should be presented in double spacing, just the same as the novel itself. A synopsis isn't a letter, it's part of the book, and editors value their eyesight.

The sample chapters – which should always be the opening chapters and not bits and pieces selected at random – will display your writing ability and style. Together, they and the synopsis will tell the editor whether she wants to see more, and she will proceed as she thinks fit.

# The draft

I'll lay my own cards on the table first. The thought of writing draft after draft fills me with horror. Quite honestly, it's all I can do to write my story once. And that is what I do. Quite a lot of what you read in my books is exactly as it was first written, without any alteration.

That doesn't mean I don't make corrections. Generally, when writing a long book, I write for several days, print out what I've done and then read it through, making corrections as I go. For a shorter book, I will usually reread every day. And it is at this point that I do most of my rewriting, if I am not satisfied with what I've already written or think the story should be told in a different way. But I don't often spend a lot of time honing and polishing my writing.

There will, however, be a number of typing errors, repetitions of words or phrases and clumsy or ambiguous sentences that weren't apparent in the first writing. I try to avoid repeating words in the same sentence, paragraph, or even on the same page, depending on the strength and significance of the word – the stronger it is, the more important it is to avoid repetition. Some should be used with care in the same chapter and some in the whole book. It is all too easy to have favourites and irritate the reader!

Sometimes it becomes apparent that a piece of action or a description would fit in better at a different point in the story, so I mark that to be moved. Sometimes the story itself isn't working, and this re-reading will show why. It may be that part of the work has to be 'unpicked' and rewritten. I once realised three weeks into a book that the balance of action between the characters was wrong, so I had to scrap all I had written and start again. Someone else reading it at that point might have seen nothing wrong, but I knew that the trend set by this particular balance would have driven the story off-course, just as a minor fault in steering a car will eventually drive it off the road.

Whatever corrections are needed, I make them before doing any more writing. This gets me back into the story. I can then go ahead knowing that – at any rate for the moment – the story is following its course.

Once the book is finished, I will push it aside and go and do something completely different. Generally, after the euphoria of the last week, when I've known how close I am to the end, there is a sense of complete anti-climax and also a real feeling of sadness and loss. I am also at the end of several weeks' or months' continuous writing and feeling quite exhausted, so a short break is essential.

Only a short one, though. I can't leave the book alone. Now I do the complete read-through, praying that I actually like what I've written. By now, the beginning and middle, written weeks or months ago, come almost as fresh as if I'd never written them myself at all, and I am often quite surprised by what I read. (This is why there is such a danger of repetition. What you may read within an hour or so might have been written with weeks in between.)

It's important to do this reading in as short a time as possible, to pick up any remaining repetitions and discrepancies. I also make a final check on dates and timings – for instance, the characters who unaccountably have two birthdays in the same year, or endure a thirteen-month pregnancy. All facts must, of course, be checked, even those you know so well you didn't bother to look them up. They're the very ones most likely to let you down. But don't leave the book too long while you make these checks. It's the reading that's important at this stage, so just make notes as you go and enjoy the story.

Not everyone works in this way. Some will finish their book, push it aside and go straight back to the beginning, writing the whole thing all over again without even looking at their first draft. Some will work over what has already been written, worrying at every word until it is exactly right. Some will do this more than once – even up to nine or ten times. And many of these are well-known, even famous, writers, so it must be right for them.

That's the point – whatever you do must be right for *you*. Whether you labour over every word in the first writing, achieving three hundred words of perfect prose each day and never touching it again, whether you rush off five thousand words that have to be worked over time and time again – or whether, like most of us, you fall somewhere in between – doesn't matter, so long as it suits you. There is no right or wrong way – only *your* way.

In any case, when your book has been accepted for publication it is more than likely that you will have to do some more work on it. Editors are not really cranky perfectionists who want to put their own mark on every book that passes through their hands, but they do read these books with an objective eye. They see it fresh – which you can't possibly do, after living so closely with it all these months – and they can quickly pick out its weaknesses and see where improvements can be made. And they'll tell you.

Don't be upset or hurt by this apparent criticism. It is entirely constructive, and intended to make a better book. Even if your editor tells you that one of your favourite characters is too intrusive – or perhaps should be jettisoned altogether – dry your tears and think about it. Even if it is suggested that the main character should take a different course of action – thus completely altering every page that follows – bite the bullet and rewrite, if only to see what happens. It may well be that this is what you wanted to do in the first place, but drew back from allowing.

This happened to me with *Black Cameo*. I brought in a character called Stephen, primarily to give the main character, Emily, someone to interact with while her sweetheart Paul was away. As it happened, they interacted all too well and, as Stephen developed into a very interesting character, so their relationship promised interesting situations. But I drew back from letting them get too close, and followed the story through to the conclusion I had already mapped out.

Here too is a classic case of plot-contriving. I didn't want to let the characters live their own story – I wanted to make them do what I had already decided. And my editor saw exactly what had happened and said, 'I think Emily should marry Stephen.'

Marry Stephen! I was appalled. That meant changing a great deal of the story from that point on (about two-thirds of the way through the book). And what about Paul, still trapped in the Siege of Paris? What was he going to say when he came home? How was I ever to get them together again?

Well, if you read the book you'll find out. When it was finished, I knew that my editor was right. I had let the situation develop and then pulled back, so that the whole episode went nowhere. Having brought Stephen in and made him interesting – and interesting within the context of this particular story – I had to follow his and Emily's story through, and let the tangles arise. And the lesson I learned from that was never to retreat from a difficult situation. Let the story twist and turn, let it become tangled and difficult. It will be all the stronger for it. And let your characters suffer – not gratuitously, but in realistic ways, in the ways that people in real life do suffer. Don't treat them with kid gloves. Your characters must experience real emotions. The summit of their happiness is in proportion to the depth of their despair.

With experience, you will come to recognise when you are taking an easy way out in a story. You will *feel* it is wrong, and even if you suppress this feeling while actually writing, it will nag you on the read-through. If you do get this nagging in your head, stop and think about making changes, even though it will make the story more difficult. Remember that this will also strengthen it.

Remember also that if there is a flaw in the story, your editor will almost certainly pick it up and ask you to make the changes anyway – and it is far better for you to do it first than to have to be asked. It might even make all the difference between acceptance and rejection – particularly for a new writer whose rewriting ability is as yet untried.

# The blurb

Many publishers like to write the blurb themselves but some ask the author to do it. The purpose of the blurb is to attract the potential reader. It tells them the story, but it also raises those enticing questions that will make the reader buy (or borrow) the book. The blurb is meant to intrigue.

So don't be afraid to let yourself go, within the confines of the two or three hundred words that you will be permitted. Introduce your main characters, give the setting and period, and put a bit of *oomph* into it – convey the atmosphere, hint at the emotion, the suffering, the joy. The blurb is a microcosm of the finished book. It should give the reader the feeling that this is the kind of book she likes, about the sort of people she can identify with and that, out of a row of similar books, *this* is the one she wants to read.

You may also be asked to write a catalogue blurb. This goes into the publisher's catalogue, which is sent out to booksellers and wholesalers and is their main way of knowing what is coming on the market and whether they want to order it. Publishers' catalogues are colourful publications, displaying the jackets as well as the blurbs, and will also be used by the representatives who visit booksellers. Obviously, what appears in these is vitally important; if you don't appeal to the bookseller, you'll never get as far as your readers.

Writing a blurb, whether your publisher asks for it or not, can also be very useful to you in the writing of the book. I nearly always write one before I start, and keep it by me throughout. It is brief enough to read in seconds and it reminds me of my original idea. The feeling of excitement it engenders is as useful as the outline itself – and can sometimes be even more useful.

I discovered this when I was asked to write a blurb for *Chalice*, the third in my Glassmakers trilogy. This request, some months before the publication date, came before I had started to write the book, or even thought much about the story itself. All I knew was that my main characters would be Cordelia and her brother Tim, who were going to be in Corning, in New York State, helping to found the new glass factory there. Somewhat hastily, I conjured up a couple of names and wrote the following:

> Timothy Henzel has inherited his grandmother Christina's
> love of glass and his father's delicate talent as an engraver;
> he dreams of creating new and innovative glasswork that will
> bring his family's firm once again into the forefront of the
> industry. His twin sister Cordelia dreams of the opportunity
> she has been given to study at Girton College, Cambridge.

The blurb then goes on to tell a bit more about what has happened before the story begins. We then come to the actual starting point, and at last there is a hint about what the book is about and what the reader can expect:

> Secretly, they steal away from Stourbridge and make their way
> to Corning, in America – known as the Crystal City. At first,
> life is hard, but Timothy soon finds work in the industry he
> loves and is given the chance to explore new techniques, and

Cordelia begins to share his excitement in this young and vibrant country – though she is forced to face her own dilemmas, not least of which is the choice she must make between two men: the American Jensen Novak, who threatens to steal her heart; and the brooding French immigrant Pierre, who brings with him a shadow of the past...

Most of this blurb is 'back–story' – events that have happened either before the story began, or very early on in the book, some of them in flashback. The blurb then goes further into the story – but not too far (remember, I hadn't really started to think about it at that stage). And the last paragraph was purely 'thin air' – I hadn't a clue who Jensen Novak was, and even less about the brooding French Pierre with his 'shadow of the past'. And I certainly didn't know at that point what choice Cordelia was going to make!

But it gave me something to work on. It was like diving off a high board on a foggy day – I didn't know what lay before me. And it was equally exciting, as I thought through the story and then, from the preceding novel, *Black Cameo*, was able to place Pierre accurately and discover just what this shadow was. From the blurb came the outline, and from the outline the full story. It wasn't all plain sailing – there was quite a lot of adjustment and rewriting to do before I had finished, and a detailed synopsis of the finished book would have been different from the one at the start. But the blurb remained the same.

# Summary

- Always send a synopsis.

- Keep the synopsis as short as possible but include all salient points.

- Don't use a synopsis to tantalise.

- Write as many or as few drafts as suit you.

- Be prepared to rewrite if your editor requests it.

- A blurb should describe the essence of the story.

- Use a blurb to remind yourself of your original idea and to keep you on track.

- Use a blurb to start you off by asking intriguing questions.

- A blurb should *always* tantalise!

# 13

# AND NOW FOR THE PUBLISHER

You've written your novel. You've felt that rush of exultation as you type the last word, and the satisfaction that comes from completing a good story, well told. You may even have felt the unexpected sense of anti-climax that often follows, when you realise that you've actually seen the last of these characters with whom you've lived for so long, that whatever happens to them next is no concern of yours... It's a bit like watching your child go out into the world without so much as a backward glance. They've gone, and they didn't even wave goodbye.

Well, they haven't really gone, of course, and it's unlikely that this is the last you'll see of them. Because now comes the business of finding a publisher and, having found one, ten to one you'll be doing some further work on the book. But we'll look at that later. Let's make sure first that your manuscript (or typescript if you want to be pedantic) is really ready to be sent out.

## Presentation

Never, *ever*, send out a handwritten manuscript. If you really hate typing, employ a typist, one who can work on a computer. Manuscripts need to be produced on a word processor these days, and more and more often need to be sent to the publisher on disk. If you haven't got a PC already, do think about it. A word processor speeds up your rate of working, makes it much easier to edit and will even correct your spelling and grammar. It's the essential tool of today's writer, and although a few diehards still swear by their own special fountain pen or lead pencil, it really is pretentious for a new writer to do the same.

You won't be helping yourself or your career. So come on into the age of technology.

Type your manuscript on one side of the paper only, in double spacing and with good margins all around. Different publishers have different house styles as far as indentation, quotation marks and various punctuation devices are concerned. If you have a particular publisher in mind it makes sense to study their house style and follow it; otherwise, don't worry too much. But do make sure you are consistent – for instance, use *either* single or double quotation marks throughout (using the alternative form to indicate 'quotations within speech') and if you use the -ize rather than the -ise endings to verbs make sure it is the same for them all. Be consistent with capitalising and hyphenating words too – in other words, wherever there is a choice, choose your way and stick to it. Some publishers will send you a set of guidelines, especially if they want you to send your work on disk. Otherwise, as long as you are consistent, these things are easily altered when the work is done on a computer. A couple of keystrokes and the whole manuscript can be re-formatted.

Insert the title of the book and your name at the top left-hand corner of each page and number your pages at the top right-hand corner. These numbers must be consecutive throughout the typescript and not start at one for each new chapter. You can, unless told otherwise, justify on the right-hand side or not, as you prefer.

Make a separate title page, including your name and address, and somewhere underneath the title – probably best on the left-hand side – say what kind of novel it is and how long. The exact word count isn't really necessary, though it's possible to give it these days, but round it to the nearest 500 words. If you use a pen name, make sure that it is clear – type it under the title, but put your real name at the top. If you are sending only a few chapters and a synopsis, say so and put your synopsis next, so that the editor can read it first if she wants to.

Don't staple sheets together. Leave them loose and put them all into a cardboard folder with your name, address and the title of the book marked on the outside. Don't bind it beautifully with the title in gold tooling on the cover; it looks pretentious and is the mark of an amateur. (It is also, so I have been told, the mark of a bad book.)

Finally, write a brief letter, asking the publisher to consider your book for publication. Say what kind of book it is – romance, historical novel, Regency, whatever – and how long it is. If you have already been published in another genre, mention that as well – a track record is always helpful. If you have special knowledge of the setting, or you think there is a special or unusual interest, tell the publisher what it is. But don't go into long explanations at this stage. If she wants to know more, she'll ask.

Enclose return postage. Wrap the whole thing up securely – but not too securely. Editors are likely to look with disfavour, if not real prejudice, at something it's taken them half the morning to hack into. And send it off, by recorded delivery for added security.

Don't forget to keep a copy, and keep back-up disks as well. Make sure they are all in the final version, so that there is no confusion when you get queries. If you have written several drafts or kept uncorrected versions, either scrap them or number them so they can't get mixed up.

## Vanity publishing

This is a trap that has been set especially for new writers, and it is a great sadness to all of us who are lucky enough to be published that so many are still caught by it.

Vanity publishing is a harsh term, as far as the author is concerned. It isn't vanity that makes us want to be published. Writers are in the business of communication. We have stories to tell and, although we may start by telling them to ourselves, we soon want a wider audience. And the audience wants us. It's a two-way process.

Vanity publishing becomes just that, however, when it allows people whose work really isn't good enough for publication to set themselves up as 'authors' for the mere satisfaction of being able to boast about it to their friends and relatives. If anyone wishes to spend their own money in having a number of books, however badly written, printed and bound so that they can give them away, they are of course perfectly entitled to do so. They could probably get it done more cheaply by a local printer, but this isn't usually what they want. They want to be able to talk about 'my publisher'.

I'm not talking here about the local historian or the family researcher who writes a perfectly good book that cannot find a mainstream publisher. Often, a local publisher (not one of the so-called 'publishers' who advertise in newspapers and magazines) will do a good job, perhaps on a profit-sharing basis. There is nothing wrong with that, provided the writer doesn't expect to make any money out of it – although sometimes a local interest book can make a profit. But the main thing is that he will get real satisfaction from it. He has achieved something that is worthwhile.

Vanity publishing becomes sheer exploitation when it encourages the writer of an indifferent novel to believe he or she has written something wonderful, or at the very least worth publishing. Often, the writer has tried mainstream publishers without success. Friends and relatives (the worst people to ask for an opinion) have all praised it, and the writer herself, having lost all objectivity – almost impossible for a writer to retain at the best of times – turns in desperation to that little advertisement aimed at 'New Authors' and calling for 'manuscripts of all kinds'. *No* recognised publisher would advertise for manuscripts – they don't need to, since piles of them arrive on their desks every day – and none of them would ask for 'all kinds'. And none of them would ask the author to contribute money towards the costs of publication.

That's what vanity publishers do. Having led you on with praise and promises – which turn out to have considerably less value than the paper they're written on – and held up visions of fame and fortune, launch parties and signings, press releases, reviews and appearances on television, they then ask you for money.

Not long ago, I met an elderly lady who told me, 'I've written a book. And I've got a publisher.' I congratulated her. But when she told me more, my heart sank. It was quite clear that this was a vanity publisher. Tentatively, I asked if she had signed a contract. No, she said. She couldn't afford it.

*Couldn't afford it!* The publisher ought to be paying *you*, I exclaimed. Haven't you tried anyone else? No, she hadn't. These people were so nice. They liked her book so much. And they'd sent her some lovely brochures.

I asked her if she would like me to help her with this. She was pathetically grateful. The sum requested had been worrying her a lot. I asked her not to do anything until I had looked at the contract. She sent me the papers. There was a definite offer to publish but no word about distribution. She was offered *much* larger royalties than any reputable publisher would offer, but only after 'expenses' had all been met. The sum they had asked as a 'contribution' towards the expense of publishing was *six thousand pounds*.

I am glad to say that the lady did not take up his 'offer', and so was spared the disappointment of being let down by the unscrupulous vanity publisher. And she most certainly would have been let down. The vanity publisher may print and bind your books and a few may even appear in shops, though it's not very likely. But wholesalers and distributors won't touch them. Nor do libraries buy them. Because all these people know that any book worth its salt will be taken by a mainstream, reputable publisher.

## Self-publishing

Self-publishing is not the same as vanity publishing. It is not really for the romantic novelist, although novels have been published in this way and have succeeded – most famously, perhaps, Jill Paton Walsh's *Knowledge of Angels*, which went on to be shortlisted for the Booker Prize. There have been other literary successes too, and a few children's books. Some people have set up their own publishing houses or presses, and offered publication to other writers. But I have to say that unless you are well-known, with a knowledge of the business and some influence with booksellers and wholesalers, you will find it very hard indeed to get your book into the shops.

Distribution is the stumbling block. It's not just a matter of waltzing into your local W. H. Smith and asking to see the manager. W. H. Smith is most unlikely to take your book – its distribution is organised from its head office in Swindon. Although the group does take a number of local interest books, it is not likely to agree to put your romance on the shelves.

Small bookshops too are likely to be cautious. You might be able to persuade one to put on a display, but the book will have to sell to justify their keeping it for long. And if it goes on to the shelves without a display, it has to compete with all the other, better-known books. It will virtually disappear. And they'll probably want sale or return terms, so even if it's in the shop you haven't actually sold it – and you might get back a decidedly dog-eared copy that's impossible to sell.

To make self-publishing worthwhile, you will have to visit shop after shop after shop – in person. You'll have to write to them, ring them up, fax them. Wouldn't you rather be writing?

As well as wholesalers, there are independent distributors who handle books from most publishers. The reps visit them as well as bookshops, and if you visit one of their warehouses you will find an Aladdin's cave of new books, bigger and better than any bookshop. Perhaps they will take over the distribution for you?

Well, you can try. I went to see one who also owns two or three flourishing bookshops in the Lake District. He showed me some books that people had sent him – lovely books, about whales and trees and local topography. They looked as good as any that I had seen in the shops. But he wasn't going to take them on. It wasn't worth it, he said. For one book, he would have to do as much work as for several books from a major publisher. There probably wouldn't be any more books coming from these particular authors. And there were already books about whales and the mountains and valleys of the Lake District. These, nice as they were, offered nothing different.

That's probably why they hadn't been taken by a professional publisher. And note that these were non-fiction, for which there may even so be a case for self-publishing. Novels are even more difficult.

Then there's promotion. This isn't so difficult – I do it anyway, whenever I have a book coming out, even though I know the publisher does it too. Sometimes it's the publisher's press release that does the trick, sometimes it's mine. But the publisher sends out review copies, which I don't do – as a self-publisher, you must. Send them to all the newspapers, magazines, radio and TV companies you think might have even the remotest interest in your book. But don't take the attitude that they've got to review your book. And don't ask for the copies back – this is just another necessary expense.

Send press releases as well, with information about yourself and your name, address and telephone number. The fact that you're self-publishing might well get you attention locally, especially if you have other local interests or connections. You are quite likely to get an interview in a local paper or magazine.

But it's a long, hard slog. And that's *after* you've done all the work of production. *After* you've found a printer to print and bind your book – or even done it yourself, if you're into desktop publishing and are willing to do whatever is necessary to turn a few hundred pages of script into a bound book. *After* you've designed it and costed it and got an illustration for the jacket. All of which is far more complicated than you might think and will consume a great deal of your time and energy, not to say money.

Again, wouldn't you, honestly, rather be writing?

If you still want to go ahead, there is a useful article written by Peter Finch, in the *Writers' & Artists' Yearbook*, who has also written a book on the subject – *How To Publish Yourself* (Allison & Busby). There are a number of others also listed, together with advice about small presses. You can even go on a training course.

At least you will know just where your money went. And any profit that is made will be yours.

## Proper publishers

Having – I hope – deterred you from ever approaching one of the 'gentlemen' of vanity publishing, and if you have decided not to try self-publishing, let's look at *real* publishers. And the good news is that there are a great many, and they are publishing more books than ever before.

Well, this isn't entirely good news: with so many books being published, it's hard for booksellers to find room for them all on their shelves. Books have a short shelf life and a book that doesn't sell quickly may be returned to the wholesaler. Worse, not only the bookseller but the publisher as well will look at the sales figures before deciding to buy your next book. But these are problems that come after publication, and there isn't much we as authors can do about them. All we can do is produce the best work we are capable of, and hope that readers will like it and come back for more.

That's our job. Marketing is the publisher's job. That's why we need them – and they need us. But in order to do the best we can for our books, it is necessary to do some homework on finding the right publisher.

There are two very useful – indeed, vital – books that every author must have – *The Writers' and Artists' Yearbook*, published by A. & C. Black and *The Writer's Handbook* (Macmillan). Both contain the names and addresses of almost all the reputable publishers in Britain, Europe and the USA, as well as those of national and regional radio, TV, newspapers, magazines, agencies and numerous other groups of interest. They also give a lot of useful advice about these and other subjects – in fact, you can find out almost all you need to know about the business side of writing from these two books.

But it is to find a publisher that most authors turn to them first. And many simply start at the beginning and work through alphabetically, which may be good news for the AA, who would be flooded with unsuitable manuscripts out of which they may pick a few winners, but a bit hard on Zomba who would only get what no one else wants.

Clearly, this is not the way to do it. The publisher you want will be somewhere in the middle. And the best way to find the right publisher is to go to your local bookshop and your library and see who publishes books of the same sort as yours. Then come home and look in your handbook for the name of the fiction editor (if it isn't given, ring up and ask, so that you can address your letter by name) and whether or not unsolicited manuscripts are accepted.

Publishers today are more and more led by genre. This has always been true to some extent – notably in crime publishing, where the distinctive jackets of Macmillan, together with Collins Crime Club – not a club at all, but an imprint – have led the field. Now it seems more the case than ever, which makes it a lot easier for authors.

Don't waste your time trying to persuade a literary publisher that it is time he started a line in romance, starting with yours. Don't send gritty wartime stories to Mills & Boon. Don't send light 'library romance' to Headline or Orion. They'll all have considered the options and decided what they want to publish. Their marketing will be aimed in the directions they favour, and there just won't be a place for something that doesn't fit in with their requirements, no matter how good it is.

Look at a number of books produced by any one publisher until you start to understand what kind he favours. If you think yours fits in, look in one of the yearbooks mentioned above to see how that publisher operates. Some will say 'unsolicited mss welcome' but specify two or three sample chapters and a synopsis in the first instance. Some – but rather fewer, I'm afraid – welcome all manuscipts. Some will say sternly that they accept 'no unsolicited mss'.

This can be dispiriting. How on earth does anyone ever get a new book read, let alone published? Well, there's nothing to stop you writing them a letter, telling them about your book and asking if they would like to see it. They just might say yes. Otherwise, the only way to approach such a publisher is through a literary agent.

## Literary agents

Literary agents act as a bridge between authors and publishers. Some authors look on agents as sharks and wolves, and no doubt there have been examples of both, but most agents are as honest and hardworking as the rest of us. They do their best for their authors because that's their job and because they love books, and they do it because they earn their living that way and the better the deal they strike for an author, the better their commission will be.

Agents live by commission. Traditionally, this has been ten per cent of the author's earnings, but some are now taking fifteen per cent and I have even heard of twenty per cent being asked, which does seem rather a lot. But then some of them do a lot for their money. And if the difference between having an agent and not having one means the difference between a small or a large advance or getting published at all – well, a large percentage of something is better than a small percentage of nothing.

An agent will read your work (most will do this for nothing but some do charge a reading fee) and comment on it. A good agent who is actively looking for new clients will do this even before taking you on, and may make suggestions and read your manuscript several times before making a decision. This doesn't mean you can use them as a criticism service, but a good agent will be able to tell if you are serious about getting published.

The agent makes no promises. She can't guarantee that a publisher will accept your book just because it comes in through an agency, but she will have a fairly good idea of its chances, and the publisher certainly takes more notice of work that comes from agents.

The agent has a lot of inside knowledge – she knows which publishers are looking for particular kinds of book, she knows when a new publishing house is about to open its doors. Sometimes publishers will approach an agent, asking if he or she have any authors on their books who might be able to write a book or series of books they have in mind to publish. (That's how I became Lilian Harry, and indeed it is how I came to be writing this book.) For this kind of opportunity alone, even though they don't come every day of the week, it is worth having an agent.

Neither the author nor the agent makes any money until a book is accepted and an advance paid. The agent will not ask you for money to assist with expenses like postage, telephone, travel and meetings with publishers, or any of her overheads. She may do a lot of work for you without being paid for a long time – perhaps, if your books don't sell, without being paid at all. On the other hand, if you shoot to fame as an international bestseller, she may earn a lot of money as her ten per cent – and you shouldn't begrudge a penny of it. Without that ten per cent being payable, you might not have the other ninety.

An agent will also take on the business of selling foreign rights (unless these are retained by the publisher, as in the case of Mills & Boon). She will negotiate large print, audio, dramatisation, radio, TV and film rights. She will agree the contract with both you and the publisher, probably get a larger advance than you would be able to get for yourself, and chase up the advance and royalties if they don't arrive on time. She will also chase the VAT payments if they are slow in arriving – some publishers are self-billing but others pay separately – and she will check royalty statements, which alone in my opinion makes her worth her weight in gold, because I can never understand royalty statements and don't know many authors who do.

An agent, therefore, is a good thing (although I must in fairness say that I do know authors who operate very successfully without one). But how do you go about finding one?

Sad to say, it is sometimes thought to be even more difficult to find an agent than it is to find a publisher. Many agents now are finding that unless an author already has a track record – that is, is already published – they just can't afford the risk and expense of taking them on. This doesn't mean they will automatically turn down an unpublished author, but it does mean that they will be choosy.

It isn't just a matter of being able to write. What both agents and publishers are looking for are writers of determination who will continue to write for years, earning a steady if unspectacular income. The one-book wonder may earn a sudden huge amount, but most of this will go in expenses and tax, leaving next year looking decidedly bare.

For the new writer, it's a Catch 22 situation. But nobody ever promised that being an author was going to be easy. All you can do is persevere. And remember, as I said before, that the number of books being published increases every year. *Some* of them have got to be written by new authors.

Caroline Sheldon has some useful advice on how to approach agents:

'Use the *Writers' and Artists' Yearbook* or *The Writer's Handbook* to spot an agent who describes themselves as interested in the type of fiction you are writing. Women's fiction covers the romantic area.

'Send a typed letter with relevant information about yourself and the book, a synopsis of no longer than two pages and the first three chapters. Enclose a stamped addressed envelope and do not expect to hear back for four weeks.

'In your letter, describe what genre you feel your novel falls into. You can use a bestselling author's name as a useful shorthand to describe a genre – Catherine Cookson, Jilly Cooper, Joanna Trollope.

'Make your material as attractive as possible both in terms of presentation (I suggest enclosing everything in a cardboard wallet file) and make the project sound tempting and something that a publisher can market in every aspect from the title you choose to your brief description of your book.'

This is pretty well how you should approach a publisher as well.

## And now you wait...

Caroline warns us not to expect a reply from an agent for at least four weeks. It might be longer. Literary agents are busy people and they have a number of clients already for whom they are reading manuscripts, negotiating rights, checking royalty statements... They attend book fairs in Britain, Europe and America, taking large portfolios of manuscripts they hope to sell. They manage to treat each client as if she is their only one, yet their lives must be like that of a juggler, keeping thirty or forty balls in the air at once.

You will also need to be patient if you have submitted your book directly to a publisher. Publishers receive enormous numbers of manuscripts every week. Those that don't come from an agent are heaped together in what is rather unkindly called the 'slush pile'. And it is only to be expected that they won't get read first. The agents have acted as a filter and sent only books that the publisher is likely to consider – it's only natural that these will get prior attention.

The slush pile does get read, though an experienced editor won't need to read the entire manuscript – she can tell from the synopsis and a quick read of the first few chapters whether it is worth proceeding, which is why you are asked to send only those chapters. But you may have to wait several weeks or even months for an answer.

This is enormously frustrating, and the only thing to do to pass the time is to start another book. Then when your first book is accepted, you'll have the second one under way or perhaps even ready to hand over, which will make a favourable impression.

If you haven't heard after about six weeks, you might write to the editor to whom you sent the book, asking if it is possible to reach a decision. This might have the effect of getting the book fished out of the slush pile and looked at; you might find that it comes back suspiciously quickly, but I can assure you that this won't be because the publisher has taken offence at your letter. Publishers are in this business to make money, not to behave like prima donnas. And if it does return with a rejection slip, at least you can send it off to someone else for another try.

## Multiple submissions

For some years, authors have been discussing whether or not they should send multiple submissions. The idea of a book being sent simultaneously to a number of publishers has been one that publishers themselves resisted, pointing out that before they actually accept a manuscript they will have already committed themselves to time and expense: discussions with the production department (which seems to wield enormous power), sales and who knows who else besides. The idea of going through all this and then finding that the author had accepted an offer from another publisher struck them as quite unethical.

I don't quite follow this reasoning. To me, it seems exactly the same as any firm tendering for a job. A builder, for instance, will spend a lot of time (and therefore money) working out a quotation for a job that will as likely as not go to a rival. Does he throw up his hands and cry 'ethics'? He does not. He just gets on with the next one and hopes for better luck next time.

I also have a lot of sympathy for the new writer, who may wait months for an answer and then find his book rejected and have to start all over again. If he is lucky enough to be accepted by only the third or fourth publisher (and remember that some now-famous writers tried as many as *thirty* publishers before finding acceptance) it could be four or five years before his book hits the shelves. Who can blame him for trying to short-circuit the system by sending off half a dozen copies of the same book at once to different publishers?

Publishers seem to accept this more readily these days, and will not usually reject a manuscript out of hand just because it has also been sent to another house. You may ask, how do they know? Current wisdom seems to be that the author should say so, in the introductory letter. Not in any threatening or cajoling manner, but simply and politely as a matter of fact. Remember, to the publisher this is business, and he will appreciate your behaving in a businesslike manner.

Agents sometimes hold 'auctions'. They only do this for books that are likely to be in high demand, and it isn't like an ordinary auction, with a number of different 'lots' – it's really more like the tender, which deals with one job and sets a deadline. The agent will send copies of the manuscript out to the chosen publishers, giving them time to read it and asking them to telephone with their offers at a certain time on a certain date. Both she and the author then bite their nails until the time comes. Then the calls begin to come in, and the hope is that the agent will be offered increasing bids, conducting business in exactly the same way as any other auction, until the top price is reached.

Generally, there is a special reason for holding such auctions. The book may be written by an already bestselling author who wants to change publishers. It may be a new venture by an established author. Or it may be an entirely new author who has produced a first novel that takes everyone by storm – such as *The Horse Whisperer,* which attracted huge interest at a book fair and sold on the strength of a few early chapters.

Sometimes authors try other ways of getting publication. I have seen the occasional advertisement in organs like Bookseller or Publishers' Weekly, trumpeting the 'novel of the year' and offering it to interested publishers. How such advertisements fare, I don't know, but I would be surprised if they achieve anything at all (unless it is an approach by a vanity publisher). Publishers simply don't need to find their books in this way. More than enough arrive on their desks, without their having to lift a finger. Their problem is to read them all.

And what if, when the answer comes at last, it is a rejection? Don't despair. It may be that you sent your story to the wrong publisher, it may be that they genuinely don't want any more books for the moment, it may be that they've just accepted another very similar to yours. It may just be that the particular editor who read your book didn't like it – it's still a very subjective business. It doesn't mean that your book isn't fit for publication. The next one might love it.

Look at the letter of rejection carefully. If it's just a standard slip, shrug philosophically and submit the book to the next publisher on your list. If it offers constructive criticism, consider taking it. The editor might well reconsider if you can correct any flaws, and even if they don't you might improve the book's chances with the next one you try. But don't make major changes unless you get a definite impression that the editor would really like to see it again. Editors are quite kind-hearted and don't like disappointing authors, so they sometimes do try to sugar the pill. Don't read too much into their words.

Don't be arrogant with publishers. They need authors, but they don't need ones who behave badly. They are *entitled* to reject your manuscript. They don't *have* to tell you why. I knew one man who (having bound his manuscript and had the title stamped on in gold) was so annoyed by his first rejection that he sent the book to a second publisher with the curt demand that it be read instantly and, if rejected, good reasons given for its rejection. I don't know what the response was, but I do know I've never seen his name on a published book.

If you get several rejections, however, it might be as well to think seriously about the book. There are, as I've already said, famous cases in which authors have been rejected many times over (crime writer John Creasey is probably the best-known) and then become household names, but these are the minority. And John Creasey was a long time ago. The market is tighter now, despite those annual publication figures. And there are few writers who actually did make it with their first novel. Many of us have manuscripts stashed away in drawers, which may never see the light of day. (Though it isn't unknown for a publisher to take them years later, when you'd almost forgotten you ever wrote them – so don't throw them away.)

There does come a time when it's probably sensible to stop submitting any book. But, if you've taken my advice, by this time you won't just be submitting one – you'll have another one on the go – or two.

---

# Summary

- Present your manuscript in the best possible way. *Sell* it to the publisher.

- Don't get caught by vanity publishers.

- Research your publisher.

- Try to find an agent to handle your work.

- Wait patiently for an answer.

- Use rejection constructively.

---

# 14

# AFTER ACCEPTANCE

## Contracts and agreements

Probably the picture most of us have is of answering the telephone one day to a summons to London for lunch – and often that is exactly what happens. Lunch with a publisher is one of the great perks of being an author. It gives us such standing amongst our friends to be able to say airily, 'Can't meet you on Tuesday, I'm afraid – having lunch with my publisher.' It has a ring of glamour about it. Swept away in a taxi to dine on smoked salmon at Claridge's or the Ritz, talking over the next book, perhaps discussing film rights, meeting the producer – there's no end to our imaginings.

The reality is more likely to be a little Italian restaurant on a streetcorner within walking distance of the office. Or even, as I once had, bangers and mash at the local pub (and, according to another author who wrote for the same publisher, I was lucky to get away without having to pay for both meals). But that isn't really the point. The point is that a *publisher* – whether the commissioning editor or the 'head of the house' – is sufficiently interested in you and your book to want to meet and talk to you. And it doesn't matter if you get lasagne instead of smoked salmon – an hour later, you won't remember a thing you ate.

Not all publishers do this. Some will simply write and say they like your book, and make you an offer straightaway. It is unlikely you will get a contract immediately – the publisher will usually want to know that you're happy with the terms set out more informally before they go to the trouble of drafting a full contract – but there will be some mention of an advance. They may also want to discuss changes and your contract may depend on your willingness to make these changes.

I would advise that, unless they go counter to some very deep feelings or principles, you make these changes. Writing may be an emotional process, but publishing is a commercial one and if you want to be published you have to produce something that people want to read. At this stage, art becomes something more like craft. If you're making furniture, you may be a Hepplewhite, with whom nobody would interfere. But it is more likely that you are a competent jobbing carpenter or joiner who isn't a great artist but can make a solid and functional piece of furniture that many people would like to own.

Naturally, publishers are delighted to come across the Hepplewhites but they are realistic enough to know that these are rare. They are pleased enough to find the carpenter who will produce good work and go on producing it, but they also know whether the current fashion is for elaborate carving or plain minimalism, and they will know if your book needs to be changed a little to make maximum impact on its audience.

I have known would-be writers who have refused point-blank to change one single word of their 'deathless prose'. Not because it's of great artistic merit (or perhaps they believe it is) but because it is *theirs*. Behaving like temperamental prima donnas, they strike attitudes, thumping their foreheads with closed fists and crying: 'But it's my *art*! It wouldn't be *me*!'

They then go back to their writers' circle and complain that publishers are heartless, devoid of all soul, and if the next one won't be reasonable they'll *pay* to have their work published. Anything rather than change one single undying word.

*Anything?* Six thousand pounds, with no promise of distribution, dismissed by bookshops, the few books that are printed (and modern technology means that these can be very few indeed) handed out to friends or left to languish in a cupboard? And this is (almost invariably) not great art or literature. It must be potentially publishable, or the author wouldn't have got an offer at all, but it isn't ready as it stands. And all the publisher wants to do is to help the author to get it up to standard.

Very, very few of us enter this world as fully-made novelists. Writing is a craft as well as an art, and it is a craft that must be learned – just as fine woodcarving, sculpture and painting have to be learned. The techniques are all-important. In fact, I would say forget about art and literature – just think about telling your story, in the best possible way to convey the excitement, the tragedy, the joy and all the rest of the emotion of it to your reader. And if an experienced editor suggests a better way of doing it, *listen* to her. *Think* about it. *Try* it. You're not destroying your original. You're not chipping a piece of exquisite marble out of existence. If you really don't like it, you can scrap it – but the chances are that you *will* like it, you'll recognise its strength and not only that, you'll add something of yourself, your own unique voice – your art, if you like – which will take the story further than the editor had dreamed possible.

And in doing it, you'll have learned more about your craft, more about writing. And even if, after having done the work, the editor still shakes her head regretfully and says it 'just isn't working for us', you won't have wasted your efforts, because you now have that extra bit of learning under your belt. And you may have given the book a better chance of being accepted elsewhere.

You may be offered a contract on the strength of agreeing to make changes, if there are any to be made, or the publisher may want to wait and see what you've done first. But let's leap on to the moment when the contract arrives – and let me say now that you should never agree to publication without having a contract with which you are happy, signed by both parties. A contract is essential to avoid any confusion later.

Authors' contracts are lengthy and complex documents. They cover all possible contingencies, from the author's name and pseudonym to electronic rights. They tell you how much advance you will receive and when – advances don't always come all at once. They tell you what royalties you will receive, from both hardback and paperback publication, when the manuscript should be delivered, and within what timespan publication can be expected, which might be up to two years. They tell you how many free copies you'll receive (anything between six and twelve as a rule) and how long the book must remain out of print before you can have the copyright returned to you. Actually, the copyright is always yours, but the contract is in effect granting exclusive licence to the publisher to publish your work. Until that licence is rescinded, the publisher holds the power.

Most contracts will cover all rights, from the first right to publish in the United Kingdom and an impressive, though unlikely, list of 'territories', to rights to publish in various other countries outside of those territories (in other words, Europe and the USA), film, dramatisation and all the rest. These will each be dealt with separately and there will be a percentage on each one, some to go to the publisher, some to you. The larger proportion should be the author's.

This is one of the areas in which a good agent is invaluable. But if you don't have one, and unless you are very conversant with these matters, you would be well advised to take advice before signing any contract, and this is where the Society of Authors will come to your aid. For more details, see Chapter Fifteen which deals with writers' associations, conferences and so forth, but for now suffice to say that any new writer can send a publisher's contract to the Society for vetting. You can, at this stage, join as an Associate Member and I recommend that you do so. If nothing else, we can be grateful to the Society for campaigning long, vigorously and, ultimately, with success in winning Public Lending Rights for authors, and if – as it probably will – your book goes into public libraries, you will probably receive more than your annual subscription, possibly for many years.

If, however, you decide to deal with your contract yourself, you do need to study certain clauses carefully. Make sure all the rights are clearly specified and that there is a definite commitment to publish by a certain date. Confirm that you will be receiving royalties – a very few publishers still offer no more than a nominal advance, with no royalties at all. They justify this by saying that they are taking a risk on a new author, which is true, and they do get your books into the libraries, as well as sometimes selling the book on for large print or paperback rights, which will be passed on to you (but confirm it in the contract). Nonetheless I still think that a royalty should be offered – if the book earns less than its advance, the publisher has lost nothing, if it earns more everyone has gained.

I have to say, though, that along with a number of other authors I started out with just such a publisher. After a few books and a number of grumbles about being able to earn as much with a short story, some of us looked elsewhere. Others continued to write happily for the same publisher for years and some may have negotiated royalty agreements. The books I wrote are still in the libraries and, after twenty years, still earning twopence every time they're borrowed. I do therefore feel a certain gratitude for having been offered that first rung on the ladder.

See that the accounting period is clearly stated, so that you know when to expect royalties. In fact, all clauses should be clear, without any ambiguity; if they're not, question them.

Question also a clause that stops you from writing for other publishers. You may be able to write three books a year – and need to, for a satisfactory income – but the publisher may want to take only one. Often, publishers don't like you writing for a rival under the same name (and there are quite sound reasons for this) so you may need to use a different pseudonym, but you shouldn't be prevented from working.

Some publishers want first option on your next book, or perhaps the next two. This sounds flattering but is not the same as a commission, when you receive an actual contract and advance for all three books; the publisher is keeping you on the hook while leaving himself free to reject you without any financial commitment. You can find yourself in a trap, with each separate contract carrying the same proviso – so you are always two books 'in arrears', as it were. If you aren't happy with the publisher after one or two books, you should be able to change to someone else, so don't accept these clauses. If you do decide to sign, follow the advice given by Michael Legat in the *Writers and Artists' Yearbook* and ensure that you are free to re-negotiate terms on future books.

## Electronic publishing

A clause that has quite recently begun to appear in contracts covers electronic rights. This is a very grey area at present. Nobody knows quite what it means – it is a term coined to cover all rights that have arisen or may arise in the future concerning publication in such forms as CD-ROM, the Internet, and so on. CD-ROM is getting sorted out, and a number of books – mainly interactive children's books, encyclopaedias, science and school learning programmes – are now being published in this form. But what of the potential of the CD-ROM to carry many hundreds of books on one small disc, for very little cost? What of the almost unbelievably cheap and easy placing of huge amounts of text on the World Wide Web? How will these affect the author and publisher of today – and tomorrow?

Nobody knows the answers to these questions, though the situation may be a little clearer by the time you read this. There are obviously great changes on the horizon and anyone who doubts this is better than the ostrich at burying his head in the sand.

I think that the potential is currently in advance of the technology – but it is the nature of technology to strive to catch up. I hear a lot at writers' conferences and other gatherings about the 'death of the book'. It'll all be on computer, writers cry, and what will we do then? What place will there be for us?

Well, the same place as there ever was, I would have thought. The place there has always been ever since Stone Age days, when the tribe gathered round the fire and listened to the story-teller. Human beings have always wanted stories and they always will. The medium isn't really that important.

Computers aren't going to write stories for us. Where would be the emotional warmth, the passion, the imagination that we've been talking about all through this book? You might be able to write a piece of software that will work out a logical sequence of events – but since when were human beings logical? And reading such a 'story' would be like listening to the voice of a robot, flat and emotionless.

I don't fear anything from computers.

What is likely to happen is that books will change. They're not going to disappear, but their format and structure may alter from being paper-based to being electronically-based. The book of the future may well be a computer, carrying several, perhaps even hundreds of books, or it may be no more than a carrier into which you can slot something no bigger than a credit card on which the book is 'printed'. But what's wrong with that? Couldn't it actually be *better*?

Imagine a computer that looks just like a small paperback book. It's no heavier, no thicker. It's flexible and pleasant to hold. It has a screen that is the same size as the page you are reading now, with print that you can adjust in size to suit yourself. (Screen flicker will, of course, be eliminated so that there is no eyestrain.) You can read it in the dark without extra light, and you can either scroll down the page – or up when you want to refer back – or perhaps touch a button and get the impression of pages turning. If you want to find a reference to a person or place, you can use the normal 'search and find' facility found on any computer today. You might even have video clips with action or scenes alongside your text, bringing the story to life as books have never been able to do. What's so awful about that?

Think about the convenience – taking such a book on holiday, with a small bundle of 'smartcards' each holding thousands or millions of words. The times when you're kept waiting and wish you had a book with you. Lying awake in the night, not wanting to put on the light to read because it might disturb your partner. Wanting to read a certain book but being prevented because you've got poor sight and it hasn't been published in large print...

These are just my ideas and may seem laughably primitive when technology really gets going. But I believe the potential is there, that we will get used to and come to prefer it, just as we do with most great changes. And the point is that *it doesn't affect us as writers*. People will still want stories. After all, we're quite happy with the other new media that have arrived during the twentieth century – radio, films and TV. None of the writers I have ever met has objected to their work being transmitted in these forms, and many write solely for them.

The other cry I hear is from readers. But we love books for *themselves*. We love to hold them in our hands and feel the shape of them, stroke covers, smell the new paper...

Granted, the physical artefact can be a joy to hold and behold. But I would like to feel that it is really the *story* that is most important, and that the medium in which it comes is of less significance.

The reason that this diatribe comes within a chapter on publishing is that nobody really knows just which way this cat is going to jump. The great problem for writers is that it is all so easy to transmit. Now, if all we were interested in were communication, story-telling and reaching the widest possible audience, none of us would be in the slightest bit anxious – we'd be thrilled that our work could be read in China at the same moment as in Lapland, without the readers having to pay a single penny towards it. But we're interested in money too. We want to be paid.

Copyright laws do not yet apply to the Internet or the World Wide Web. It is difficult to see how they *can* be applied. CD-ROMs can be made and copied at minute cost and are ridiculously cheap to distribute. Work can be copied and pirated and there's not a thing we can do about it.

There is comfort, however. At present, it doesn't seem to be happening. Books are being put out on Internet, but generally as experiments with both the author's and publisher's agreement – and they're mostly in the genre of science fiction, the theory being (I assume) that most computer and Internet buffs are going to be science fiction readers. So – no threat to the romantic novelist there.

I can't really see any point in anyone pirating books on the Internet. It's still too cumbersome. We are still having to sit at our desks to 'log-on', or at least have a laptop with built-in modem and mobile phone. A book is a huge amount of text to download and print out, and you have to pay for your paper – it would probably be as costly, if not more so, as buying the book. And at the end of it, you'd have a great fat bundle of loose A4 sheets instead of a neat paperback.

As for CD-ROM, cheap and easy though it may be, there still has to be a market – and it seems unlikely that anyone is going to go to even that much trouble to pirate work by new and unknown writers. In any case, books are already pirated in some countries that don't recognise international copyright agreements, and we have lived with that for quite a long time.

Whatever the new problems may be, they're ones we shall all have to face together. Why not use the new technology positively, rather than worrying about negatives that may never happen? Web space is cheap and readily available now. Use it to publicise your own work. Put on your own 'catalogue' – a list of every book you've written, with jacket illustrations, a blurb and an extract or two. When you get reviews, quote from them. Put on a short biography of yourself if you want to. Advertise new books. Say who the publisher is (and tell them you're doing this). Some publishers will even be pleased for you to put on an order form that can go straight to them. I know of several authors who have sold their books overseas in this way, finding markets they otherwise would not have reached.

If you're an Internet subscriber and get free Web space from your server, you can soon learn to use it. The HTML commands that give you 'hot-links' – the ability to jump from one page to another, following a certain track – are easy to use. Forget your worries about the death of the book – it may undergo a transformation, but the story will never die – and let the world know you're there.

## Copy-editing and proofs

You've got your contract, duly signed by both parties. You've carried out any changes the editor suggested, and she's happy with them. All you have to do now is bank your advance and wait for publication day.

Not quite. There is often still work to be done, and by signing your contract you will have agreed to do it. I speak now of two more occasions on which your book will return to you: copy-editing and proofs.

Even though you have made changes and checked all your facts, there may still be queries from the copy-editor. This person reads your manuscripts before it goes to the printer. She will read it twice and perhaps three times, and in so doing she may find a number of anomalies, repetitions or points that require clarification. She might suggest splitting some paragraphs, or running others together. She will look for inconsistencies – not only those thirteen-month pregnancies, but details such as the spelling of any words that may have two acceptable versions, words italicised in one place and not in another and so on. She will make notes for the printer.

You don't need to worry about printers' marks, of course, but you will need to read through the copy-edited manuscript carefully in order to answer the queries, confirm facts and correct any problems. Remember that this is the last version before proofs and everything should be in good order – don't think you can wait for the proofs before making amendments.

It's a good idea to ask your editor what the schedule is for your novel. Once a publication date is set, she should be able to give you an idea of when the copy-edited manuscript is likely to arrive, and when you will be expected to correct proofs. You can then set aside the time required.

This is important, because although the contract usually stipulates a time of about three weeks for these tasks, more often the publisher will want them done in about a week. At the same time, it is both polite and businesslike to let your editor know when you are likely to be away from home, so that she doesn't send you any major jobs then.

It's helpful if both parties adhere to this policy. I once discovered two sets of proofs in the coal-bunker, left there by a helpful postman while I was away on holiday. Considering that I was away for a month and it was the middle of summer, there wasn't much chance of them being found, read and returned in  time for the printer. They were read in-house and there were no snags, but I felt very uneasy about them. An author indemnifies the publisher against such things as possible libel suits, and there's always the faint chance that something has crept in that you would have taken out!

Apart from that admittedly less likely possibility, it's very annoying to open your newly published book and discover, on the first page you look at, a typo that you would *definitely* have spotted. (The fact that you can read proofs half a dozen times, including backwards as one author I know does, and *still* find a typo on the first page you look at is neither here nor there.)

Proof-reading is one of those tasks that an author likes to talk about. 'Can't come tonight, I'm proof-reading.' It reminds everyone of your exalted status. It has a certain cachet that isn't there when you say you can't come because you've got to finish your year-end accounts. I find proof-reading a curious blend of pleasurable discovery and mind-bending tedium.

This is because when I send off my manuscript I have no idea at all whether the book is a good one or not. I've lived with it for several months, from conception to delivery, and if I'm not actually sick of it

I'm certainly glad to have it over and done with. I'm also very relieved that I've actually managed to finish it and that the six hundred pages or so of typescript are there on my desk rather than a figment of my imagination. Not only that, I'm usually exhausted and would have difficulty in being objective about the *Beano*, let alone my own outpourings.

Some of my energy has returned by copy-editing stage, but I'll normally be deep into another book by then and it can be faintly irritating to have to break off and check facts I was sure of in the first place, or worse still put right that overlong pregnancy.

But when the proofs come, it is like a sign that this really is going to be a published book. Although they're still loose sheets of paper, they *look* more like a book. The pages are printed and numbered exactly as they will be in the finished article. And if you've already half-forgotten the details of the story, it will read much more like a book that someone else has written – you will be able to look at it more objectively. And it's very nice indeed if you find yourself enjoying it.

That's not the reason you get proofs, though. The idea is that you check them through to make sure there are no typesetting errors. I live in hope that as it becomes more common for authors to send their work on disk, which will already have been checked, so this stage will become unnecessary, but I don't think it's very likely. Whenever work is done on a script, the potential for mistakes exists, and proof-reading will always be an important part of producing a book. And it really is necessary for the author to do it, for her own satisfaction. I haven't forgotten my unease over those proofs in the coal-bunker.

So why the tedium? Well, that comes from having to read proofs at least twice. Better still, get someone else to read them as well – someone who can spell. If you can't spell yourself, this is essential because you just won't recognise all the mistakes. And I've found that, even if I have help, the second reader will invariably find mistakes unnoticed by the first.

Proof-reading is done with a series of margin signs that tell the printer what the error is. Publishers will send you these if you need them, but you will find them also in the *Writers' and Artists' Yearbook*. Errors made by the printer are signalled with red ink, errors that are yours (and be honest about this) with black or blue. Now is *not* the time to make alterations to the plot, to dialogue, characters' names or anything else. All that should have been done long ago. It could cost you quite a lot of money to do it now, as your contract will probably stipulate that you should pay for any corrections over a certain percentage. Once the proofs have gone back, you really can sit back – or, better still, go back to the new book – and wait for publication day, the trumpets and the champagne.

Unless you are very lucky or a brilliant new talent, this probably won't happen. Some publishers do send their authors a bouquet of flowers now and they will try to arrange some local publicity, such as an interview in the weekly paper or on local radio, but that's about all. Not that it's to be sneezed at, of course, and remember there's nothing to stop you banging your own drum a bit. But don't expect publication day to be marked by anything much more than your own celebrations. Buy yourself some champagne. Go out to dinner. Have your own launch party, if you like. Why not?

You've had a book published. You *deserve* an accolade.

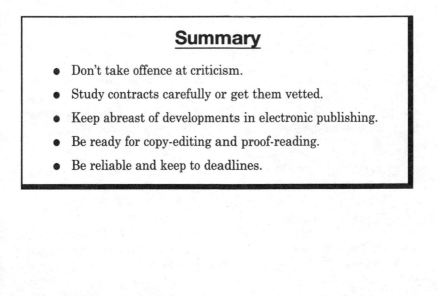

## <u>Summary</u>

- Don't take offence at criticism.
- Study contracts carefully or get them vetted.
- Keep abreast of developments in electronic publishing.
- Be ready for copy-editing and proof-reading.
- Be reliable and keep to deadlines.

# 15

# BUSINESS MATTERS

Once you begin to earn money from writing, you will have to declare your income to the Inland Revenue and you may even get involved with VAT. You will find more detailed advice on all these matters in the ever-useful *Writers' and Artists' Yearbook* and *The Writer's Handbook*. The Society of Authors also has a number of leaflets explaining the various special circumstances applying to authors, what can and can't be claimed as expenses and so on. But in general, it's just a matter of commonsense.

## Income tax

Don't try to get away with *anything*. Everything you earn will be declared by those who pay you, so don't try to hide it or 'forget' to declare it. That includes money made from selling books (authors don't do this much, but it sometimes happens – though you need your publisher's blessing – at writers' conferences), and from talks, workshops, creative writing classes and so forth. Declare expenses paid to you as well, and then claim them back – it sounds cumbersome but keeps the figures right and nobody is in any doubt as to which is which.

Normally, income is counted in the year in which you receive it. But sometimes a writer is allowed to spread a large advance over several years – sometimes carrying back, when the book has taken a year or more to research or write, sometimes forward in the case of advances that are paid several years before the book is written. For instance, you may sign a contract for three books, receiving an advance separately for each, but you will receive, say, a third for each one on signature of the contract. This can make quite a large lump of income in one year, even though the second and third books will not be written in that year. With the Inspector's agreement, you can carry forward the relevant amounts to the years in which the books are written, making a more logical calculation possible for your income tax and possibly keeping you in a lower bracket for those years. But don't forget to include it when the time does come! (And don't forget to save the money, which you'll need as income during those years as well as eventually paying the tax.)

Remember that you are allowed to reduce your tax bill by claiming 'allowable expenses'. These can be quite varied. In my time, I have claimed for wear and tear on walking boots, rucksacks and cagoules (when I was writing a series of walking books), as well as the more usual stationery, postage and travelling expenses. I claim a percentage of the household heating and lighting bills, since I work at home, and it is also possible to claim for special 'office' furnishings such as bookshelves, filing cabinets, desk and chair and so forth. Any costs that are incurred solely and wholly in respect of your business are clearly allowable as deductible expenses. If they are incurred only partially for business (like my walking boots), make a proportionate partial claim. My feeling is that if you are reasonable in your claims, the tax inspector will be equally reasonable.

Some things, such as computers and printers, and your car, are what is called 'plant'. You can't claim for large expenses like that all in one year, so they are written down over a period of time. This is where many of us do need professional help. A good accountant really can be a good investment, or your bank may be able to help.

Travel can be a big expense. My accountant once asked me to justify a trip to America, through California and Arizona to the Grand Canyon. Why did I decide to go there? he asked. Had I actually written a book about the Canyon? Did I have to take my husband with me, and did I think that I was justified in claiming for his expenses as well? He added that he himself did not doubt me but he needed my justification in order to be able to talk convincingly to the inspector.

An experienced writer who had been through all this before advised me that a writer 'has to be able to look for experience'. How would we write if we never went anywhere? Especially with the kind of book I was writing then, the Mills & Boon romance, which so often depended on a foreign setting – and, being the kind of writer I am, the necessity of seeing it for myself.

I pointed out that, for me, seeing a place was essential before I could write about it. I also wrote better if I were really interested and enthusiastic about the subject. The visit to the Grand Canyon was undertaken simply because I wanted to write about it – the idea of it excited me. Yes, I enjoyed the trip and looked on it as a holiday as well, but I was definitely collecting material for a book.

Yes, I did have to take my husband with me. Travelling alone in the USA, especially driving long distances, just wasn't an option. And his expenses weren't that high, anyway – accommodation was mostly charged by the room, not per person, and the hire car cost the same however many people were in it.

As for having written the book – at that time, I hadn't. I'd started one, sent off a few chapters and been rejected. I didn't think that this should prevent me from claiming the trip – or part of it – as a justifiable expense. Meanwhile, I'd been commissioned to write the Glassmakers Trilogy, and other writing had to be put on hold for a while. But in any case, I'd undertaken the trip on good faith, I'd started the book, and I couldn't be held responsible for the publisher's decision that it wasn't right for them at this time. Just as, if I'd written it and it hadn't earned its advance, this would have been a factor beyond my control and I must still be able to claim the expense of writing it as a loss.

I was pleased when both my accountant and the tax inspector accepted this argument and I have never had any other problems or queries. I was even more pleased when, a short while later, I did write a Mills & Boon romance set in the Grand Canyon and it was accepted and published (*Hidden Depths*).

Play straight with the inspector and he – in my experience – will play straight with you.

## Value Added Tax

A business that has a gross annual turnover of (currently) £47,000 a year must register for VAT. A business that has a smaller turnover is allowed to register. If your income comes into that bracket but fluctuates, as it probably will, from year to year, you will probably be assessed at having a registrable income.

If you think you are going to come within the realm of VAT, register *at once*. If you don't, you will have to pay all VAT due from the period when you should have registered – and you won't be able to go back to your 'customers' – in this case, your publishers – and claim it from them. You'll have to pay it yourself. That's apart from any trouble you might get into for not complying with the law.

Anyway, VAT can be a good club to be in. It means that you can claim back the VAT due on many of your expenses, such as stationery, office equipment and so on, so all those supplies come cheaper to you. You have to do the office work, of course, send invoices if the publisher isn't self-billing and keep careful records, but there really isn't much to it, and having to update everything quarterly does keep the less business-minded amongst us on our toes. You can get ledgers in your local stationer's that make it self-explanatory, and the VAT office will help if you're uncertain.

Don't ever worry about it. I am amongst the least business-minded authors, and towards the end of each quarter I start to fret until finally (usually at the last moment) I get down to it, and it takes about an hour.

## Public Lending Rights

This is a very useful source of income – as long as you remember to register your books. You must do this by the end of every June, registering each book published during the preceding year – books registered earlier don't need to be re-registered. Different editions of the same book, such as hardback, paperback, large print and so on, should be registered as well. The form from the PLR office in Stockport will explain how to do this.

Public Lending Right was created in 1979 and it is paid out of a sum allocated by Parliament each year – in 1996/7 it was £500,000. This pays for administration costs and reimburses local authorities for the costs of recording loans in sample libraries. The libraries themselves are regularly changed, so that each part of the country is represented at some point – if you've written a book of particular and limited local interest, you may get nothing for years and then receive a sudden windfall when your local library takes its turn. (But don't try to take advantage by borrowing your own book every day for the entire year, because the system is designed to notice this!)

At the time of writing, authors get about two pence each time a book is borrowed. But to prevent the really popular authors from walking off with all the money, there is a ceiling of £6,000, which is a very useful sum to most of us. Usually about 100 or so authors qualify for this payment. There is also a bottom limit of £1, which will at least buy you a newspaper in which you can search for jobs, and there are several grades in between. Around 25,000 authors are registered in any one year, and by far the greatest number receive between one and ninety-nine pounds.

Children's authors are the Cinderellas of this system because school libraries aren't included. It is to be hoped that this may somehow, and before too long, be put right. It is also expected that PLR will soon be extended to reference books that are used within libraries.

PLR applies only to books in British libraries. Other countries run similar systems, but we cannot benefit from them and neither can foreign authors benefit from their books being borrowed from our libraries. Authors must be resident in the United Kingdom or in Germany to qualify, since there is a reciprocal arrangement with Germany, which is administered by the Authors' Licensing and Collecting Society. Members of the Society of Authors are automatically included in this arrangement. Otherwise, apply direct to ALCS. Addresses are given in the Yearbook.

PLR must be declared to the income tax inspector but it is outside the scope of VAT, so does not have to be included on VAT returns.

## Copyright

Copyright is a very complex subject but, basically, everything you write, as soon as you have written it, is protected by copyright law.

This means that no one else can publish your work and claim it as theirs, and if they want to quote you they must ask permission and, if you demand it, pay you. Likewise, you shouldn't quote anyone else in your work without similar permission.

There is a rule that up to 400 words can be quoted without permission, for purposes of criticism or review. But I would never quote in a book without first clearing it with the owner of the copyright.

Copyright in a work lasts for seventy years after the death of the author. This has brought back into copyright a number of works that had previously come out. So if you want to quote from anything written by an author who died fewer than seventy years ago (and this includes poetry and songs, which are probably the most-quoted works) you will have to trace the present owner of the copyright – an heir or estate. The Society of Authors may be able to help here. For more advice on copyright issues, see The Writers' and Artists' Yearbook and The Writer's Handbook.

When writing *Moonlight and Lovesongs,* I wanted to quote from the song 'As Time Goes By', from the film Casablanca. I didn't even know who had written it, but I was able to trace the writer through the Internet by looking up the film, and I then approached the Performing Rights Society and discovered who held the copyright. I finally found myself talking to a man in London and we negotiated a fee for my inclusion of four lines from the song in my book. It isn't cheap – though they did agree to reduce their first figure – and you might decide you don't really need to include the quotation after all! But it's cheaper than being sued after the event.

There is no copyright in a title, which is why a huge number of quotations, part-quotations and sayings get used as titles. So many have been used, in fact, that some people think we'll soon run out of titles – but Shakespeare and the Bible, two of the favourite sources, will be a rich vein to mine for a long time to come and new sources are being created every day.

Some new authors worry that their work is in danger from someone in a publisher's office who will see what a good idea they have and steal it (returning the manuscript as a reject). Nobody can say that this will never happen, but I think it is unlikely and besides that, none of us will ever be published if we are too paranoid to send our work out. It's a risk – and a remote one – that we have to take.

# Societies

There are a number of societies that are useful to join, the two main ones for romantic novelists being the Society of Authors and the Romantic Novelists' Association. Each operates in a different way and you might like to join both eventually, though if you aren't yet published you will probably start with the RNA.

## The Romantic Novelists' Association

The Romantic Novelists' Association was inaugurated in 1960. Its first President was Denise Robins and she was supported by two other well-known romantic writers, Barbara Cartland and Netta Muskett. The Chairman was Alex (Vivian) Stuart, who later wrote a number of robust novels about the early emigrants to Australia. The membership at that inaugural meeting numbered 115 and the aim was to raise the standard of romantic writing amongst its own membership by making an award for the 'Best Romantic Novel of the Year', an award that is still made.

The RNA does more than reward its published novelists, however. Through its New Writers' Scheme, which it claims is a service not offered by any other national specialist writers' association, it will read and criticise manuscripts from unpublished authors, give advice and even forward the best ones to publishers. The scheme doesn't guarantee success, and the RNA does not act as an agent, but many writers who have been published and are successful today speak with great warmth about it and say it has helped them. 'Probationer' members may join for up to five years, provided they send in at least three manuscripts during this time.

The RNA holds meetings, runs seminars and weekends and sends a quarterly newsletter to all members, keeping them in touch with each other and with trends. It also holds an annual Lunch at the Café Royal, in London, with a prominent speaker and the presentation of its Award for Best Romantic Novel of the Year and New Writers' Award.

The fee for joining the RNA is £12 a year. Apply to Jean Chapman, 3 Arnesby Lane, Peatling Magna, Leicestershire. LE8 3UN.

**The Society of Authors**

The Society of Authors was founded over a hundred years ago. It does not operate as a guide but as a trade union. Full membership is restricted to published authors, but those who have a manuscript accepted can become Associate Members.

The Society provides information about agents, publishers and others concerned with the book trade as well as about such matters as income tax, libel, VAT and so forth. It will advise on negotiations, vet contracts, take up complaints on behalf of members and pursue various kinds of legal action. It holds meetings, conferences and seminars so that authors can meet and discuss all the many and various matters that interest them about their work, and so that they can improve their own conditions and those of other authors. For instance, the Society was instrumental in achieving PLR, campaigned vigorously for the Minimum Terms Agreement which now forms the basis for many publishers' contracts, and keeps a watchful eye on the ever-present threat that VAT may be imposed upon books.

Not only that, the Society operates a retirement benefit scheme, pension and contingency funds and a number of other benefits. It is well worth joining, and I recommend that you do so as soon as you are eligible. The annual membership fee is £70, or £65 by direct debit. Apply to The Society of Authors, 84 Drayton Gardens, London SW10 9SB. Tel: 0171-373 6642.

## Conferences and courses

I am always astonished by the number of writers I meet who are unaware of the various writers' conferences that take place up and down the country. Once you have been to one, you will find out where and when some of the others will take place – and if you are in the huge majority, you will be hooked and anxious to go to the next.

'Conference' is rather a solemn word to apply to these writers' meetings, although a lot of conferring and exchanging of ideas and information certainly takes place. But all those I have been to have been enormously enjoyable and have brought me real friends. I owe much of my own success to such conferences and the stimulation and encouragement I have found there.

## The Writers' Summer School

Known to all those who have ever been there simply as 'Swanwick', this is my favourite. It takes place during the middle of August at The Hayes Conference Centre in Swanwick, Derbyshire, and lasts for six days. These six days are packed tightly with courses, workshops, discussion groups, talks and surgeries, as well as two main lectures each day from visiting speakers. Recent speakers have included Beryl Bainbridge, Mavis Nicholson, Lynda Lee-Potter, Celia Brayfield, Simon Brett, William Horwood, Deric Longden, Dannie Abse, Roy Hattersley, Tim Waterstone - the list goes on. Swanwick is now in its fiftieth year and counts equally illustrious names amongst past speakers.

It sounds like a hard working day. But to writers, who work so much in isolation, it is a joy to be able to work with each other, to exchange ideas and gossip, to talk with others of like mind, and simply to enjoy each other's company. Every minute between sessions is marked by groups of writers scattered about the rooms and gardens of the Hayes, all busy making the most of their annual 'fix'. And in the evenings, there are impromptu parties springing up everywhere, not to mention the entertainment which we provide for each other – the concert, the dancing, the pantomime...

*Pantomime?* In *August?* Of course – written by members and performed by others, to the huge delight of the rest.

Swanwick can accommodate nearly 350 members, in rooms ranging from adequate (in a large garden shed that was once the headquarters of the Health and Beauty movement and went on to house German prisoners-of-war) to luxurious, in a new block with en-suite accommodation. The price reflects these differing standards but because all writing events other than the two daily main lectures are drawn from the body of the membership, and are not paid for, the cost is kept very low.

To enquire about a place at Swanwick, write to Brenda Courtie, The New Vicarage, Parsons Street, Woodford Halse, Daventry NN11 3RE.

## The Southern Writers' Conference

Open to writers from all parts of the country, the SWC is held on a weekend during June at Earnley Concourse, near Chichester. Earnley is a purpose-built centre with comfortable en-suite accommodation and excellent food. The weekend is run on lines similar to Swanwick, and there are always several well-known speakers, including such names as P. D. James, Anne McCaffrey and Frank Delaney. Earnley is known for its peacocks, which emit unearthly shrieks during lectures (and halfway through the night too) and have given rise to several plots for murder stories (usually involving the murder of peacocks).

Write to Lucia White, The Old Stable, Dorking, Guildford for information about Earnley.

## Other Courses

There are a number of other such weeks and weekends, including the Writers' Holiday (an ironic title if ever there was one) in South Wales, and the South-Eastern Writers' Weekend at Bulphan, Suffolk. Most run on similar lines. The Writers' Holiday runs during the last full week of July in the luxurious students' village at Caerleon College, The University of Wales. Past speakers include Susan Moody, Iris Gower and Jessica Stirling. Write to D. L. Anne Hobbs, 30 Pant Road, Newport, South Wales, NP9 5PR.

To apply for a place at the South-Eastern Writers' Conference, write to Carol Cannavan, 10 Dury Falls Close, Hornchurch, Essex RM11 3AX. The accommodation is all ground-floor and en-suite, with an indoor swimming-pool, and again you will find courses, talks and discussions as well as lectures by such writers as Maureen Lipman, Jack Rosenthal and Terry Pratchett.

All of these residential weeks and weekends are worth going to, not only for the courses and lectures that offer so much, but for the exchange of information, ideas and general rapport between writers. Many writers – myself included – believe that we would not have progressed so far in our writing without this stimulation.

## The Arvon Foundation

The Arvon Foundation began in 1968, offering writers of any age over 16 and any background the opportunity to live and work with professional writers. With three main centres, one in Yorkshire, one in Inverness and one in Devon, the courses cover poetry, narrative, drama, writing for children, songwriting and the performing arts. Courses are residential and last for five days. There are resident tutors, and participants also spend time working alone. I think the emphasis is more on the literary than the 'popular' novel, but this is not to say that a romantic novelist would not find help and stimulation there. Bursaries are available to help those on low incomes.

Write to The Arvon Foundation, Lumb Bank, Hebden Bridge, West Yorkshire HX7 6DF.

## Writers' Circles

If you can't get to a weekend conference, or just don't want to, you may still find it worthwhile to join your local Writers' Circle. These meet anything from weekly to monthly and usually operate by hearing and commenting on each other's work, or sometimes by setting writing tasks. The level of criticism varies and you may have to be selective in which advice you choose to take, but in general it can be very useful. I have belonged to several, in different parts of the country, and have always enjoyed and benefited from the contact, the advice I have received and the friendships made.

Information about Writers' Circles can be obtained from Jill Dick, who has compiled a Directory of Writers' Circles. Write to her at Oldacre, Horderns Park Road, Chapel en le Frith, Derbyshire SK12 6SY.

Writing can be a lonely business. It is not just that you are sitting on your own for hours every day, living with a set of people who don't really exist. It's also that you can't really discuss them, and the problems you have with them, with your friends and family. Like everyone else, you need to meet with people of like mind, who are on the same wavelength, who know what you are talking about and will sit happily for hours, late into the night if necessary, just talking 'shop'. You need to know that you aren't, after all, rather peculiar.

Or, if you are, that there are plenty of others who are peculiar too.

## Summary

- Be honest with the tax inspector...
- ... and the VAT man.
- Register for PLR.
- Join an appropriate society or association.
- Take opportunities to meet other writers.

# 16

# AND FINALLY...

## The last word

So that's it. There are a hundred other things I could have said, and if I were to write the book again next year there would be more, because by then I hope I'll know more. There is always something to learn and good writers never stop. But I hope I've given you enough to get you started.

And once started, to keep going. You must keep on trying. Elizabeth Warne (author of *Ragtime Girls*, *Wild Silk*, etc.) agrees: 'Never wait for inspiration,' she says. 'On the days when you feel totally unable to write, press on. These may be the days on which you do your best writing.'

So approach your writing with determination – but not *grim* determination. Remember always that you are writing to entertain. Romantic novels are not meant to bring home the hopelessness of human existence. They are there for enjoyment, for escapism, for learning a little about humanity, for learning about love and understanding. When you find people looking down their noses at you because you write romance, tell them this, and don't be ashamed. There is nothing to apologise for in writing about the impulses that affect us all, about the mainspring of our existence.

You are writing for people to enjoy. And the way to achieve this is to enjoy yourself. Fall in love with your hero, think of your characters as real, living people and care for them as you would your own family. Give them the best that is in you and you will be giving your reader the best as well.

You will surely reap your reward, in the satisfaction of writing and completing your book, in the pleasure of seeing that first, brand-new copy and spotting it on the shelves of your local bookshop. And, most of all, in those letters that begin, 'Dear ..., I have just finished reading your book and I felt I must write and tell you what pleasure it has given me...'

Then you will know that you have written a truly romantic novel.

---

# And what not to do...

- *Don't* send a handwritten or badly typed manuscript.
- Never, *ever*, get involved with vanity publishing.

A couple of tips from Celia Brayfield, in her book *Bestseller*:

- Do not expect anyone to care as much about your book as you do.
- Do not think badly of anyone who cares less about your book than you do.

And one last one from me:

- *Don't give up.*

---

# FURTHER READING

*The Making of a Novelist*, Margaret Thomson Davis (Allison & Busby)
*The Craft of Novel-Writing*, Dianne Doubtfire (Allison & Busby)
*How To Write Historical Novels*, Michael Legat (Allison & Busby)
*Writing Step By Step*, Jean Saunders (Allison & Busby)
*The Craft of Writing Romance*, Jean Saunders (Allison & Busby)
*How To Write A Synopsis*, Stella Whitelaw (Allison & Busby)
*Bestseller*, Celia Brayfield (Fourth Estate)
*To Writers With Love*, Mary Wibberley (Buchan & Enright)
*Research For Writers*, Ann Hoffman (A.&C. Black)
*The Shell Book of Firsts*, Patrick Robertson (Ebury Press)
*Our Secret Names*, Leslie Alan Dunkling (Sidgwick & Jackson)
*The Guinness Book of Names*, Leslie Dunkling (Guinness Books)
*Dictionary of Historical Slang*, Eric Partridge (Penguin)


## Societies in North America and Australia

The following societies may also prove useful to potential authors.

Australian Society of Authors
PO Box 1566, Strawberry Hills, NSW 2012, Australia

Authors' League of America, Inc.
330 West 42nd Street, New York, NY 10036, USA

Romance Writers of America
13700 Veterans Memorial, Suite 315, Houston, TX 77014, USA

Canadian Authors' Associaton
PO Box 419, 27 Doxsee Avenue North, Campbellford, Ontario KOL 1LO

# INDEX

# THE CREATIVE WRITING SERIES

What makes a good story into a publishable novel or a creative vision into the next award-winning screenplay? In this series, experienced authors in a wide range of creative writing genres share their knowledge and expertise to help aspiring authors find their voice. All the books in the series demonstrate how to develop ideas into a saleable form and give plenty of opportunities for practising newly acquired writing skills along the way – from the germ of an idea to a finished work.

## <u>Titles</u>

*Creative writing*

*Screenwriting*

*Writing a novel*

*Writing for children*

*Writing poetry*

*Writing erotic fiction*

*Writing a romantic novel*

*Writing fantasy and science fiction*

*Writing crime and suspense fiction*

*Writing essays and reports*